Film at Wit's End

By the same author

Metaphors on Vision
Film Biographies
Brakhage Scrapbook
I . . . . Sleeping

Film at Wit's End

EIGHT AVANT-GARDE FILMMAKERS

Stan Brakhage

DOCUMENTEXT
McPHERSON & COMPANY

FILM AT WIT'S END
 For information, address the publisher: McPherson & Company, Post Office Box 1126, Kingston, New York 12401. Book design by Bruce R. McPherson. Typeset by Word Management Corporation. Manufactured in the United States of America. First edition.
1 3 5 7 9 10 8 6 4 2 1989 1990 1991 1992

Publication of this book has been assisted by grants from the literature programs of the New York State Council on the Arts and the National Endowment for the Arts, a federal agency.

Library of Congress Cataloging-in-Publication Data

Brakhage, Stan.
Film at wit's end : eight avant-garde filmmakers / by Stan Brakhage.
p. cm.
Filmography: p.
Includes index.
Contents: Jerome Hill — Marie Menken — Sidney Peterson — James Broughton — Maya Deren — Christopher MacLaine — Bruce Conner — Ken Jacobs.
ISBN 0-914232-99-1 : $20.00
1. Experimental films — United States. 2. Motion picture producers and directors — United States — Biography. I. Title.
PN 1995.9.E96B74 1989
791.43'028'0233—dc20
[B] 89-32072 CIP

Grateful acknowledgment for permission to reprint the following materials in this book: For excerpts from *A Long Undressing* by James Broughton, published by The Jargon Society, copyright © 1971 by James Broughton, by permission of the author. For excerpts from *The Fly in the Pigment* by Sidney Peterson, copyright © 1961, copyright renewed 1989 by Sidney Peterson, by permission of the author. In addition, the publisher wishes to acknowledge with particular gratitude the assistance of Mr. and Mrs. John Schofill for making available original tape recordings from which these essays were adapted, and for their hospitality; the help of Nadia Shtendera at Anthology Film Archives in locating and providing film stills; and the skill of Hollis Melton for photographing five films especially for this volume. Other photographers contributing stills and portraits, via Anthology Film Archives and the author, are Francine Keary, William R. Heick, Mike Chikiris, Joel Singer, Joseph Rostin, and Robert A. Haller. Finally, thanks to the editor of this project, Kathleen Hamel Peifer.

The paper used in this publication meets the minimum requirements of American National Standard for Information Sciences — Permanence of Paper for Printed Library Materials, ANSI Z39.48-1984.

This book is dedicated to
Helen Lerchen,
without whom it would never have existed.

CONTENTS

Film at Wit's End

Introduction

From 1969 through 1981 I traveled back and forth, every other week, from my home in the Colorado Rockies to Chicago at least one semester, sometimes two, each year, to teach at The School of the Art Institute. These essays are adaptations of lectures originally intended to help students to understand the films of these makers, which were shown at appropriate moments midst the spontaneous "text" of my speaking and entertaining questions. The alternate weeks, when I wasn't present, longer films were shown, films were reviewed and so forth. When I came to class, I made every effort to arrive in a state of meditative excitement, so that I could share with the Art Institute students my experience of each of these men and women I was lecturing about with the most intelligent enthusiasm I was capable of transmitting — so that the films could be seen as closely as possible to the creative process in which they were made. The audience was almost always reciprocal in its enthusiasm. We had very little time together, three hours every two weeks, and we made the best use of it we could.

It is as difficult to describe the aura of excitement that prevailed at The School of the Art Institute across the 1970s as it is to recreate in words the lives of the filmmakers, their various milieus. During the period when these lectures were given, the school was, essentially, a series of hallways fronting a railroad yard at the back end of the Art Institute itself. The halls and classrooms were grubby, often cold and always noisy. In the late 1960s the faculty and student body had joined together and picketed the Art Institute for their rights, with the result that, for some time afterward the school was essentially governed by a faculty/student coalition. Mayor Daley had singled it out as an alternative to reform school for some of the less dangerous juvenile delinquents. A kind of gentle anarchy reigned, then, at the rear end of one of the greatest art museums in the world. I think the administration then was comprised essentially of Dean Roger Gilmore, aided by someone who handled the "economics." There were, I believe, never more than three secretaries, one of whom was a veritable "mother" to the students, even letting some of them sleep on her apartment couch when they had been evicted from their flats. Another secretary, I remember, had taken a deep interest in filmmaker Gregory Markoupoulos, and was one of his most ardent patrons over the years.

It was my old Boulder friend Tom Mapp, who had some kind of administrative position there, who conceived of the idea of flying me into Chicago every other week for these classes, and who later collaborated with Dean Gilmore and me to hire George Landow and John Schofill to be the school's film department. All this was done quite informally and with consummate ease.

My classes were so huge in enrollment (one semester, as many as 450 students), that they were held in the main auditorium of the Art Institute itself, Fullerton Hall. Architecturally, Fullerton Hall is the epitome of the nineteenth century — Chicago's nineteenth century. All of us were affected by its faded but dignified glory. It suggested, at every turn of baroque-rococo, the highest aspirations of mid-country America, and it invited a discipline which softened even the most raucous teenager. Every belligerent question that was asked — and there were many — was echoed solemnly; every assertion I made, similarly. The auditorium itself demanded loud applause if one was pleased and the stoniest silence if not. Obviously, I cannot translate this atmosphere into a book. The worst of the fact is that a book cannot show the films; and the films — as well as their being understood and appreciated — were what these classes were all about.

I lectured on the whole history of cinema. But when I began to speak about contemporary filmmakers I had known, John Schofill was induced to record the lectures, which he then continued to do across most of the decade. Meanwhile, back in Denver, my dear friend Helen Lerchen, having heard some of the tapes, was determined to transcribe six of the lectures included here — a task so rigorous and exhausting that I am abashed at her belief in my talks. Without her, this book would never have been dreamed. Then came my task of turning spoken language into readable text; then of sending each of these texts to those filmmakers who were still living — Broughton, Conner, Hill, Jacobs and Peterson — so that factual errors could be amended and biographical "bones" picked and realigned. There is a foot-thick pile of letters and exchanges in this matter. Then more years went by before Bruce McPherson learned of the material, and got excited enough to publish it in book form, slightly expanded from the original manuscript. His editor, Kathleen Peifer, put it in final order, as well as politely but firmly prompting me to "flesh out" two of the essays with yet more detail and formal adjustments. But these essays remain essentially as they were delivered (sometimes combining two or more lectures) across the years of teaching at Chicago's high time of spirit and dedication to the arts. All people mentioned in this introduction – including all the students I came to know in my course of teaching – are my friends: this book comes to exist along a line of friendship. Though we've never met, I presume to call Kathleen Peifer my friend also, because she has edited in such a way as to keep my voice alive, and even at times echoing in Fullerton Hall, within the book.

Many of the filmmakers have died since these talks were given. Maya Deren, whom James Broughton called "the mother of us all," was dead before I even began to teach. Marie Menken and Willard Maas died within four days of each other, Marie going first and Willard unable to continue without her. Jerome Hill had barely completed the final version of his autobiography, "Film Portrait," when cancer gripped him. He is the only true "gentleman" I have ever known. His death seems the end of a particular human style: I am grateful there was time to get something of it in film. Christopher MacLaine lingered on for many years in a nursing home; Willard Morrison finally managed to get some of his film royalties to him by simply going out and buying him a great many necessities to ease his life there in the last years.

But the others, I'm happy to say, are very much alive in every sense of the word, despite the increasing neglect of film as an art, as something made by human beings creating very much as we expect from artists in all other media. These people continue to make new films very much as they always have, which is to say that they make each new film as a marvelous evolution distinct from all previous work. Even Sidney Peterson, who had said he was finished with filmmaking, was prompted, with the assistance of Marjorie Keller, to create a new work several years ago.

It is my hope that these lectures, now printed, will at least encourage people to take advantage of the new marvels which these, and all other dedicated film artists, are now making.

— Stan Brakhage
Boulder, Colorado
February, 1989

Jerome Hill

With Jerome Hill's work we encounter wit at its sharpest and at the same time, probably, its gentlest in the history of art.

Now, we will have to try to define "wit." Usually, when we speak of "wit" in the European sense, the French come first to mind. (When one says, "English wit," one puts the emphasis on "English, to differentiate it from European wit in general.) Wit, by its nature, is a humor that does not evoke laughter – the laughter that wit usually gets is a politic "ha-ha-ha." Wit is sharp and based in repartee. It is a statement in relation to a fact, a fact in the immediate environment or a fact in history or in one's own experience. Wit points out those things in life that are disturbing or incongruous. I think of wit as a pointer in the hands of a prestidigitator standing before a blackboard in a seventeenth-century French drawing room prodding someone's fat belly or pretentious hat. Wit is rapier-like and sharp in a way that can verge on black humor. In fact, when you take wit from Paris to Vienna, it slurs into black humor; whereas in England, it becomes broadsword stuff.

In America, with our English heritage, we start with broad humor. We get our humor straight from the Pilgrims. We're still trying to laugh down our Puritan uptightness. (An excellent example of this American brand of wit is in one of Chaplin's greatest shorts, "The Pilgrim," in which Chaplin plays the preacher.) The American starts with broad humor, but is inclined to sharpen it although not in order to pierce. American humor is greatly influenced by a sense of sport which, as with the Greeks, is almost a religion. On the other hand, Americans are known as a cruel people. They can be cruel in a diplomatic way, just as the French are; but there is also the sense of the foolish American doing more harm by attempting to do good and screwing everything up over and over again. The American inherently struggles to be gentle and at the same time not to be taken advantage of.

Jerome Hill's work epitomizes this American wit for me better than any other artist in this century. I think this is true because as a child he met all the American contradictions at their most superficial level.

Jerome Hill was born in 1905. His grandfather was the famous empire-builder, James J. Hill, in all ways the exact opposite of "Joe Hill," the great worker's symbol, a man who was martyred by just such a man as Jerome Hill's grandfather. Jerome recognized perhaps better than Joe Hill himself the evils of the American railroad-building era, the wrongs that were done by the railroad barons in destroying and robbing the economy. Yet, he came from a wealthy family of railroaders.

His mother descended from the Dutch colonizers. This side of his family had known power but its power was dying out, so they were interested in something more in life. His mother was the strong, happy influence, without the problems and guilt of the nouveau-riche. The conflict between Jerome's mother and the rest of his family bore a tremendous influence on his life, and one can say it balanced and shaped all of his work. Jerome has said that, even as a child, he understood that the rest of the family made his mother continually miserable because they were jealous of her, jealous of her sparkle and her search for other values than merely maintaining the railroad empire. Of course, his mother and father were in love, so there was that balance in their life together; but the power of the grandfather, James J., was enormous. He was not only an empire-builder, but he shaped many of the attitudes and ideas of his time.

James J. Hill started in the steamboat business, then gave that up and began railroading because he had an overwhelming idea. The idea was not original with him, but his was the power that gave it shape. He believed that people should move east and west across America, rather than north and south. He thought that people should move along a line of shared weather, a line which he believed would make communication among people easier because they shared the same kinds of food and clothing and so forth. If they moved north-to-south and south-to-north, he believed, they would cross lines and climatic barriers, and this would only interfere with efficient communications. His idea influenced not only the railroads but the highways of the nation. It is much more difficult to travel overland from Canada to Mexico than it is from New York to San Francisco which is a longer distance; and this is largely due to J.J. Hill. He was an influential old bastard.

At the time when Jerome was growing up, all the rich families were concerned that their children have "culture," so they saw to it that the children were given music and painting lessons. But when the Hills discovered that Jerome was genuinely interested in painting, they were horrified. In his great autobiographical work, "Film Portrait," there is a scene of Jerome at about the age of ten, which records a moment of one of the deepest humiliations of his childhood. The scene itself was shot by a Hollywood cameraman who had been brought to the Hills' home to photograph the children and their activities. This was how the rich made their "home movies." So the Hills decided with some sad unintentional subconscious demonism to photograph little Jerome painting. Jerome, of course, loved painting, but he was not permitted to have his own painting shown in the film. Instead, his family hired a professional painter to paint a picture to be put on the easel, and Jerome was to hold the brush and pretend to be working at it.

Still, Jerome went on with his own painting. The main courses of study he followed through school in America were painting, music and architecture. When he went to Paris, it was as a young American painter. Film came into his life in those days as a kind of game or amusement; people were beginning to fool around with their home movies as 16 mm cameras became available.

Although many filmmakers begin with painting, Jerome is the only filmmaker I know who has also studied music all his life — music in its full range. Almost all the music in his films is his own, including the 1930s jazz. Only on those parts of his soundtracks where one hears the scratch of a phonograph needle, indicating a period piece, is the music not his own.

Jerome has worked in many fields. In the late 1920s he published the very first book of photographs without any words other than the title, *My Trip to Greece*. He is also an architect, although he has designed houses only for himself and friends. Beginning in the late 1920s, he wrote books of poetry, one of which is titled *Haikus*. The poetry in *Haikus* is based on the classical idea of the Japanese haiku, an extremely difficult and highly structured form.

With bowed heads a group
Looks at something on the ground,
An old umbrella.

The standard haiku form is 5-7-5, 17 syllables with five to the first line, seven in the second, and five in the last. Haiku poets make some very fine and wonderful combinations with this form. They will draw an extra syllable out of a word or drop a syllable in order to achieve the form; and yet the ultimate idea of the haiku is to conceal the 5-7-5 mechanics of it, so that the reader is aware, not of the form itself but of the image which the poem paints.

My glasses are lost.
Tonight, tonight finally I
Shall hear the opera.

In the second line of this haiku by Jerome, the "ly I" is slurred as one syllable to meet the seven-syllable demand, and in the last line, "opera" is pronounced in two syllables, "opra."

Imagistically, this next one is very like the Japanese haiku:

High above the lights
Of Times Square a lighted clock
Higher still the moon.

You read Jerome's poetry, you look at his short films, and you're reminded that when something looks simple and appears to have been accomplished easily – such as hand-painting on film – it is only the most concentrated and disciplined art that makes it that way.

A passage from a letter that he wrote to me, about the quality of paint he used to portray a fire in a fireplace in a particular painting, gives a good idea of his knowledge and discipline in making art:

> As you realize, the nap of velvet is vertical to the plane of the cloth, unlike other woven fabrics. It thus partakes of the quality of the texture of the center of a black-eyed susan or the short fur of the rabbit. The highlight along the thigh of a man dressed in velvet as painted by Titian or Van Dyke is thus not at all on the high surface of the thigh where it would be expected to be, but along the outermost edge. A satin-clad thigh gets the highlight smack down the center. Holbein toys with these two fascinating opposites. A sleeve cuff in satin with its brilliant center-located accents will protrude from a dark velvet cloak whose few highlights, the only area that in fact indicates the color of the garment, will be only faint outlines of the folds of the texture. . . . Velvet glows, while satin sparkles or shines. Now, my open fire was of the glowing variety. A flame in it would have to have been handled differently; satinly. Now, you suggest that I might have used a special type of paint for the velvet niche. No, it is oil paint; a deceptive term anyway, as nearly every color in good quality oils has an individual chemical makeup and is made from a divergence of elements: animal, vegetable and mineral (unlike all current commercial colors which are coal tar and will all some day turn to gray).

Now, it was a revelation to me that almost all commercial "oil" paints are made from coal tar and that practically all of the paintings painted in this century will turn to gray. In order to get paints that will not fade out, one must seek out and buy extremely expensive paints. Parenthetically, I'll add that Jerome also informed me that nearly all paper manufactured in the twentieth century will turn to dust within a hundred fifty years: that almost all books published in this time will completely disintegrate.

Jerome continues in the letter:

> If there is any magic or alchemy it is that I laid on a layer of vermilion first and scraped it with a knife; after it was dry . . . I scraped over it a layer of crimson. Vermilion is made of mercury and sulphur, strictly mineral, and the crimson I used was vegetable, from the roots of the garance plant. I left the highlights on the inner corners of the niche for fear that the results would be satiny. Then . . . the final gesture was to scrape again. . . . One touch of a palette knife, but a very frank and bold one, scrapes away everything superficial and leaves an honest and interesting color surface that for some reason stands for an inner conversation between the material, the subject, and the artist, that the brush strokes were concealing.

Jerome Hill has stayed true to those forms of painting that he discovered when he was younger and which are truly his great metier. He has not tried to keep up with any market or trend. He has remained true to a form of painting which is not now looked at unless it is signed by Bonnard or some other artist of the late nineteenth century; and this is tragic, because we have great artists – Jerome being the supreme example – working in the styles that are true to impressionism, painters who have developed that form without in any sense imitating it.

Jerome possessed great gifts as a child, as most artists show signs in childhood of something that sets them apart. Nearly always in men it involves a particular attachment to the mother. In many cases, the mother has a prophecy of some sort that the child will be extraordinary. For instance, a gypsy or midwife told Freud's mother that she had given birth to one of the world's great men. Such things aren't said to every mother, and every mother who hears such a thing does not necessarily take it seriously; but those who do sometimes rear great men. In Jerome's case, I surmise that he got his strength from his mother, especially when the rest of his family wanted to stop him from painting.

The most gracious thing the old grandfather said when someone was kidding him about the fact that Jerome was becoming a painter was, "Well, three boys. One for the railroad, one for the bank, and one an artist." So they had Jerome tabbed very early.

Another thing that set Jerome apart was his health. He had a classic case of hay fever, as well as serious thyroid trouble. His family told him that this was evidence of overcreativity, in a way that seemed to him to say, "Stop creating so much." Jerome told me that these physical conditions "gave me a funny crutch to lean on. I think it was the only reason I was never psychoanalyzed." (Freudian psychoanalysis was fashionable among the upper classes at the time.)

In "Film Portrait," a period of about ten years in Jerome's life, between the ages of ten and twenty, is completely left out. That is the thyroid period. Thyroid problems can cause one to lose or gain weight suddenly. Jerome would lose weight and be a bean pole, or he would get chubby and pear-shaped. He had a dream, a hope, that the condition would remedy itself; nonetheless, he was put through an excruciatingly painful operation on his thyroid gland, which did not cure the problem; but in about his twentieth year, it went away, much as Jerome had dreamed it would.

It is particularly pertinent to comment on Jerome's wealth, as it has been fashionable in this century to believe that if you only have money you can do much better than you have been doing. Certainly, many artists say, "Alas, if only I had enough money to eat I could survive." And it is true, there are artists who have quite literally died of malnutrition in this country — I've known some. The literal statement on their death certificates says "malnutrition," and this in the United States, the richest and fattest country in the world. So there has always been this powerful illusion that if an artist could just make enough money — what couldn't he do! But in knowing Jerome all these years and studying his life, I have come to the conclusion that wealth, if used against creativity, can kill a young artist more quickly than the worst poverty.

Jerome suffered in his family, and he suffered in the art world because of his family's wealth. Early on, in Paris, when he was painting, he was accepted for a show with one gallery. He took some of his paintings to this gallery, and they were excited about doing a show for him; so he brought over the rest of his paintings, and they became more and more enthusiastic. But one day, they confronted him with, "You did not tell us that you are the grandson of James J. Hill — that you are from the Hill family. We could not possibly give you a show, because if we did everyone would think that your family had bought the show for you and there would be no way for us to convince anyone otherwise. Our reputation would be ruined." Again and again in his life, Jerome encountered this sort of problem.

In his own family he was tabbed as the black sheep, and therefore the monies involved in his inheritance were tied up in such a way that he could not dispose of them "foolishly." He could travel, stay at the best hotels and spend money on himself, but the family lawyers had arranged things in such a way that he could never make donations of his funds to help artists or people whom he might want to help, or contribute to charities of his choice, or things of that sort. Most American wealth is tied up very carefully so that if a budding St. Francis should arise in the family he is stopped in his tracks. In fact, were such a one to take off his clothes and throw them at his father's feet, he would probably find himself in a madhouse forthwith, and for the rest of his life.

For Jerome, money became such an agony that he almost insistently never had any on him. Or he would crumple up ten- and twenty-dollar bills and thrust them into his pockets; then situations would arise where his credit cards were useless and he would search through his clothes frantically for some wadded-up bill that had probably been through the laundry several times.

I remember, most poignantly, an incident when he visited me in Colorado in the mid-1960s. He stayed for several days, and we had a wonderful time talking and looking at paintings and films. The time came to take him to the airport, and as it happened, I left the house without any cash on me, which I realized after I'd driven into a gas station. So, without thinking, I turned to Jerome and said, "Jerome, you're going to have to pay for this because I don't have any cash," just as I would have said to anyone under the same circumstances. Suddenly, we were in the middle of one of those most terrible moments. First a look of shock came over Jerome's face, then horror, fear, embarrassment – and then complete confusion as he started searching frantically through his pockets. His initial shock came from his thought that I was hitting him for money, as often happened to him with other artists. His next reaction was of horror at himself for having thought that of me; and then the instant he realized that it was a flat, honest need for cash at the moment, he panicked for fear that he didn't have any on him, either. It was such a terrible moment that, after I had analyzed what happened – which took a little time – I said to him, "Look, I'll never ask you for money again."

Money becomes something quite else, something totally different in this context, and it can operate more viciously than poverty. In Jerome's generation, people in this country could usually struggle to get themselves out of poverty; but it is not true that any sensitive good person who happens to have money has it better than any sensitive good person who happens not to. Wealthy people have their own horrors, and one of them is in their relationships with other people, especially with people who are not wealthy.

The problem is that if you have money and someone who does not asks you for some, it could become an endless proposition. Two people of about equal wealth (or poverty) can lend to each other and borrow or give, because it's not an endless thing. There is a limit. There is no limit — rather, there can seem to be none — when one friend is wealthy and the other is poor. It's like the story of the man who had a custom every Christmas to give his newspaperman ten dollars. Every day the newspaperman would hand the paper to the man through his car window, and at Christmastime he would receive his ten dollars. This had been going on for many years, when one year the man came to the newspaperman and said, "I'm sorry, I can't give you your Christmas gift this year. My son has just started college, and it has taken all the money we have. We're not even going to have much of a Christmas this year ourselves, because all our effort is going to put our son through college." The newspaper man exclaimed, "Putting your son through college? On *my* money?"

Money has interfered with the acceptance or recognition of artists more often than not. Yet, great things result from this social hangup on money in curious ways. For one thing, in Jerome's case, we have his great "Film Portrait," a portrait of the world of wealth by an artist who lived in it and grew up in it, and we have no other film like it. In all Jerome's works we see some total understanding of that world and his life within it. For another, wealth prevented Jerome from entering into that struggle always to be creating the "latest thing." Jerome went his own way because he had to fight against his family and their pressures, not the "trends." He gained the strength to be himself very early, and he was never influenced by other art movements unless they were meaningful to him. He maintained with beautiful dignity older styles of art and made them grow considerations of tradition that very few artists or art mavens water and feed these days.

"Film Portrait" is an autobiography in the sense that it deals explicitly with Jerome's most personal life's relationship to film. It draws on film clips taken in his childhood and his whole childhood involvement in art and life. It comes closest to any kind of filmic answer to Proust.

An autobiographical work is a difficult work to undertake in any art form. Mark Twain, for instance, had promised one of his close friends that he would write his autobiography if he could do so honestly. He said that in the whole history of the world's autobiographies he had found very little honesty, and if he could write his own honestly he would do so proudly and happily. Several years later, his friend wrote to him, asking where the autobiography was. Mark Twain admitted that he had found it impossible to write honestly, so he had thrown it away.

Hill's "Film Portrait" is a startlingly true autobiography, true in every sense — open and clear and at the same time a recapitulation of the history of film itself. That history begins with paintings, stills, other kinds of images that came before film and predicted film. It begins with every conceivable childish and stupid use of projection possibilities — the projectionist through the centuries, cutting up and happily so, home family entertainment and shadow plays, etc. Jerome recapitulates these senses by his use of the footage that was taken of him as a child in 35 mm. This offers a sense of what was actually film's most gross beginnings, all the mistakes, the happy side of them, the interesting part of them and the completely corny photography showing stupidity so beautifully. He shows this in his own work as he gradually builds up to the little fragments of masterpieces that remind us of Millet, and his own interest in documentary work which begins with the Lumiere films. In fact, as Jerome began his first film experience with camera in hand, he took some films in the same place where the Lumiere brothers did. The Lumieres were very important to Jerome, as indeed they were to the whole development of documentary film. He was filming in the station at La Ciotat, the station where the first publicly released motion picture was shot. The Lumiere brothers, who were still alive at the time, were sitting there, so they may have seen the young man with the camera.

I think that Jerome may have actually intended "Film Portrait" to be more shocking than it is today. The changing attitudes of our times have helped to balance his wit. All his friends and his family who first saw this film and saw him shaving himself must have been horribly embarrassed and shocked that he would do such a thing – that he would shave himself in public. It would be like someone in a later generation filming the birth of a baby and showing the film in public.

Jerome had always been under that kind of pressure from his family, and he really would have had to worry about whether he was doing the right thing in showing himself shaving in public. Then to put it in the negative as he did was to make the act grotesque to his generation. But Jerome knew exactly what he was doing. He knows exactly the tenor of the wit he is producing; you see this when he takes a bottle in a color negative sequence and puts shaving lotion on his hands, and some of it drops into the bowl. You see him again, and his face has gone from a green to a blue to match the blue of the shaving-lotion bottle. That quality of wit with color is the exactitude whereat I am most sure he is conscious.

Jerome shares with me the sense that the subconscious is supreme in making a work of art, if one has the courage to follow the directions of the subconscious in spite of what friends or family or anyone else says. The subconscious creates the balance. We are talking here, not only about our inner personal feelings, but the insight that comes when we strip away personality and go down deep into ourself, beyond genders and subcultures, and find that we are touching all people in our culture; then more deeply, stripping away all personality, until we arrive at the universal – the unconscious that is shared by all of humanity. This is the step at which the province of art truly begins, when one touches all men and women of all time. The mistake that so many people make is to aim for that consciously and directly — it's a mistake that is especially common in Hollywood. They say, "We will just aim this film so that it touches all people of all time," but all they ever really manage is to touch the current fashions and whatever the popular paranoia is at the moment; and ten or twenty years later the movie is embarrassing even on the late show on TV.

I have been to art shows time and again where one of Jerome's films was thrown in with a number of others, including mine; and afterward people do not remember the Jerome Hill film, consciously. That would be a rather sad statement except for the fact that, really, art is for the subconscious; and sometimes the subconscious can make more use of it when consciousness doesn't interfere. Often, art can serve to bring the conscious and subconscious together. This was one of the great drives of Jerome's art.

In "Film Portrait" Jerome makes two references to "the present." One is "The Me That Am," which is fractured English and was even more outrageous in the French version of the film. Later, he takes up what "the present" might be. These constitute two interesting philosophical statements; but they are not Philosophy in the sense that one receives it in a college course, nor are they cracker-barrel philosophy. They are the philosophy of wit, very close to Voltaire.

"Film Portrait" begins in 1910; many things about it are technically innovative and were invented by Jerome, such as hand painting on negative. In the film he calls this "a very old technique." When I looked at the film with Jerome, I asked him, "Jerome, why did you say that? It's a new technique." He thought about it and realized that he had forgotten he had been the first one ever to paint or draw directly on the film. There had been hand-painted film before that, but only for color effect, never any hand painting or drawing on the strip of film in any intelligent way.

"Film Portrait" is, I believe, the only direct autobiography we have in film. There is Jonas Mekas' "Diaries, Notes, Sketches," which is diary but not autobiography in a strict sense. We have Cocteau's "Blood of a Poet," "Orpheus" and "Testament of Orpheus." One could say that this last is autobiographical, but it is also allusive and poetic; whereas Jerome's "Film Portrait" is a very straight attempt to present autobiography on film. Of course, subsequently, James Broughton's "Testament" and my own "Sincerity & Duplicity" series of autobiographical films were very much inspired by Jerome's "Film Portrait" as well as by Jonas' "Diaries."

A few years after Jerome had been forced to pretend to paint someone else's painting for the professional home-movie photographer, at a time when he was attending a military school in St. Paul, he painted an extraordinary mural on the walls of the school, "Great Men of the World." He was a teenager when he painted it, and the theme of great men of the world seems to have portended his future interest in biography. He wanted to film certain great people while they were alive, to get something of their life story on film. The people he chose were Grandma Moses, Albert Schweitzer and Carl Jung. He also made a short film called "Schweitzer and Bach," which deals with Schweitzer's ability to play Bach with such deep understanding.

Jerome spent a great deal of time photographing Jung; I believe his were the only moving pictures that Jung permitted to be taken of himself in his home at that time of his life. The film, however, was never finished; we know of many artists who have entered into a religious area and failed to complete their work in it, and yet with Jerome Hill, we find qualities of Jung in every one of his films.

One of the most perfect examples of Jerome's "religious art" is his film "Canaries." Within its brief life on the screen, this film creates archetypes from the most simple daily surroundings. Is there anything more unlikely to stir the romantic soul than a caged canary? A dripping faucet? But by the time this film has worked its spell, it is "the lovers" in it who seem to be submerged in dailiness — except for the fact that they are gripped (literally, by paint on the film) by the architecture of the spell of canaries, seen as never before.

Jerome's interest in Carl Jung influenced some of his most greatly underestimated films. He made two feature-length dramatic films in 35 mm which opened in New York. Although they are emotionally quite opposite to James Broughton's "The Pleasure Garden," they are related to the Broughton work in that they are another of those films which ought to be liked and appreciated popularly but are too much of an art to succeed in the American market. The first film is "The Sand Castle," about a little boy who is taken to the beach with his sister and is left there. He builds a gigantic sand castle, and all the people on the beach gather around and become involved, some against what he is doing but most of them for the boy. One way or the other, they are all very excited about the boy's sand castle, and when the tide begins to come in, they all become disappointed and horrified. It begins to rain, and the little boy is left alone. There follows a dream sequence which involved much hand painting. This sequence is in color, whereas the rest of the film is in black and white. The dream sequence takes place inside the sand castle, and is very much inspired by Jung's basic philosophy. Then the sea comes in and washes the castle away as the little boy watches. He is not saddened at all; he is delighted.

Jerome's first short film was "Anti-Corrida." In the early 1950s he had received an Academy Award for his very fine but standard documentary on Albert Schweitzer. (The clip of him receiving the award, from Cyd Charisse, is in "Film Portrait.") After he received this award, he met Jonas Mekas and thereby became aware of the independent film movement in America. It was within a very few years after that, that he produced "Anti-Corrida," which drew him to the attention of other filmmakers as an artist.

There are three titles for this short film. The first was "Anti-Corrida"; the second was "Death in the Forenoon"; and the third was "Who's Afraid of Ernest Hemingway?" These titles exemplify a pattern in Jerome's thinking that is important to understanding his work. First, he makes his bitter statement against bull-fighting,

"Anti-Corrida," the strongest he could make, with a pun wrapped in. Then he feels that perhaps it is too strong, too French, too European, and as he is about to release it he softens it to "Death in the Forenoon." But that is too broad, too English, too mean for the wit of the film, so he balances it with "Who's Afraid of Ernest Hemingway?" All three titles are important to consider because in all Jerome's work and throughout any of his films, his wit dips up and down this scale: "the sharp hit" (which may seem more sharp to him than to us), "the broadsword" and, finally, "the American flat."

Jerome went to France when most of the "lost generation" of Americans went, perhaps a little later, and he finally managed to secure a home in Cassis. He spends all the time he can there, but has to come back to America to do his work and fulfill his other obligations. He is American to the core, in mannerisms, habits and so forth, and it is his American sensibility which has served to shape the wit in his works.

His films constitute a high and unusual art. I say "unusual" because it is fashionable to reject the whole arena in which Jerome Hill works – as a painter, a filmmaker, an architect and a poet – as not being modern, as not being saleable in the fast turnover of the New York or world market. His is a very high art that is difficult to see, just as D. W. Griffith's has always been difficult to see.

But the fact remains: Jerome Hill's films are great because they are poised on wit and achieve a balance – a gentle, intentional, particularly American balance.

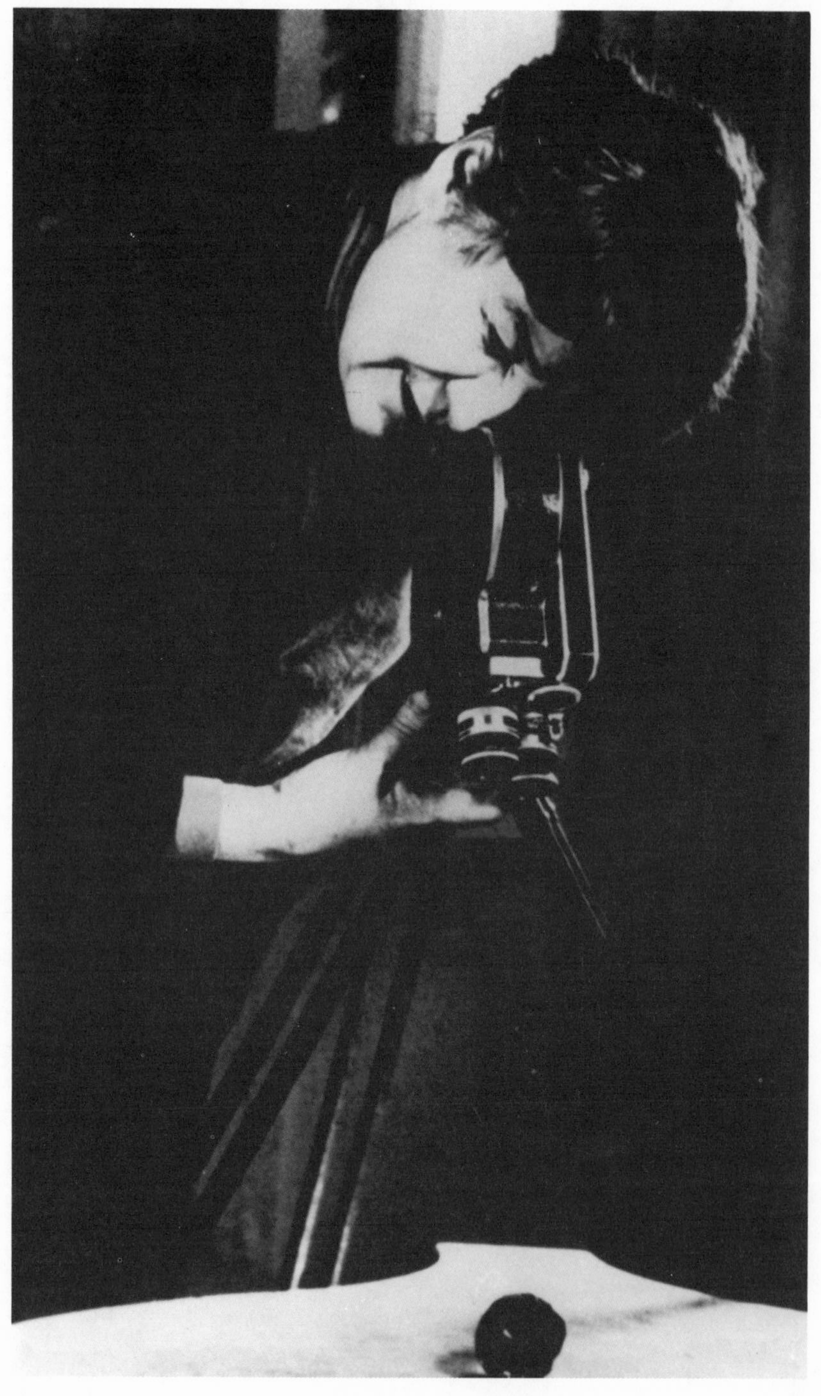

Marie Menken

I came to meet Marie Menken in the mid-1950s, when the filmmaker Willard Maas and his then-lover Ben Moore invited me to look at some films at Willard's Brooklyn apartment. Willard was one of the most ostentatiously gay filmmakers in the New York art world at the time, and he and Ben were in the midst of a tumultuous affair; they were also making a film, "Narcissus," which Ben was "starring" in. When I arrived at the apartment, Marie was there. She was an enormous woman, easily six feet, two inches tall, with broad and solid shoulders, a surprisingly slim waist and stout but shapely legs, like a dancer's. Her public wardrobe tended toward tailored suits and blouses with clusters of ruffled frills at the neck, but the night I met her she was dressed as she usually was "at her full ease" — in a flouncy but tattered lounging gown. Her size and attire, along with a series of elaborate gestures with her large hands, made for a formidable entrance.

Now, I knew that Marie was a painter/collagiste and that she was involved with film. Two things I didn't know that evening: how much her work would come to inspire mine over time; or that she was married to Willard. The latter I found out soon enough when Willard introduced her as his wife. He always introduced her that way — as "my wife" — which Marie would always smile at. She had one of the most beautiful smiles I've ever seen.

Our film-viewing evening went along pleasantly, until the projector was turned off. Then Ben and Willard got into a violent argument and started hitting each other, right there in front of me, the virtual stranger, and Marie. Before I knew what was happening, we were all out in the hallway, Willard and Ben screaming at each other and running down the stairs with me and Marie running after them, trying to grab Ben away from Willard. Finally, Ben kicked Willard down the last flight and out the door, and left him beaten and bleeding in the snow.

Willard wouldn't let us touch him — he insisted on getting up and stumbling off, trying to find Ben and make it up. I was shocked, shaking like a leaf. I'd never seen anything like that before. And there I was, after Willard had staggered off, alone with Marie, whom I barely knew at all, feeling that I should comfort her somehow and completely unable to do anything. But it was Marie who turned to me, explained what was going on, very straightforwardly, and comforted me about it — she, as I learned, whose heart was forever torn.

Marie was born in 1910 in New York City to Lithuanian immigrant parents. She had a brother, Joe, and two sisters, Helen and Adele with whom she remained close. Before she met Willard, she worked as a secretary for the Guggenheims in order to support her work as a painter. Her paintings were of a style which did not in any sense become fashionable until the late 1950s and 1960s; so she did not achieve any widespread fame for them in the 1930s. But she was respected in the New York art community, and in the mid-1930s she received a residence-grant from the Yaddo art colony in upstate New York. Willard Maas also received a Yaddo grant, as a poet-resident, and the story goes that they met in that idyllically set art colony.

Willard was born and reared in California, the youngest of five sons of a German immigrants, the railroad magnate Christian Maas and the famous suffragette "Baroness" Von Kroll. He had come to New York in the late 1920s — or, as he used to put it, he "fled" to the east coast — where, by the 1930s, he had become fairly well known as a poet. He was also very active in left-wing politics, and had been married, briefly, to another left-wing activist with whom he had one son, Stephen, in 1935, before they were divorced. Then he met Marie.

Marie and Willard became very close very quickly, and got married in 1937, when the world was still struggling out of the Depression. Somehow, they managed to get a rent-controlled penthouse apartment in an old Brooklyn building – and they managed to hold onto it right to the end of their lives. The penthouse was a fantastic affair. It was as if the *Flying Dutchman* had been shipwrecked on the top of an apartment house, and the various fragments of it had fused together so that these two extraordinary people could inhabit it.

Marie got pregnant fairly soon, and it was while she was pregnant that Willard discovered he was a homosexual and started off on what would be come a very strenuous gay lifestyle. But Marie could not bring herself to leave him. First, she was Catholic, so divorce, for her, was out of the question. And, too, as she often said, she "loved him, all the same."

Her greatest heartache was not Willard's coming out of the closet, it was the still-birth of their child. She once told me that the loss of their child sent her into such a terrible depression, that one night she pulverized their wedding rings between two stones and hurled the pieces from their apartment. Yet they lived together all the rest of their lives – not out of some rationally reached agreement, but because they continued to love each other deeply, even though they were arguing, bitching, fighting, screaming at each other constantly. And living in this mad and incredible penthouse from which the landlords were always trying to evict them.

Marie and Willard had the most lavish parties in the art world that I ever was invited to. They had turned that outlandish penthouse at 62 Montague Street into a famous – sometimes notorious – salon of artists, literati and various and sundry illuminati. They would include everybody – Marilyn Monroe and her then-husband Arthur Miller, Charles Addams, Reinhold Niebuhr, Truman Capote and Andy Warhol, to name only a few. One of their closest friends, who was in regular attendance, was Richard Wright, at the height of his fame after the publication of his *Native Son*. They would also go out of their way to invite "characters." I remember one party when Marie pointed out a bedraggled, blousy, rich old lady flanked by two young, accommodating men. "There she is," Marie said, "the Medea of the Twentieth Century." When I asked who the hell the Medea of the Twentieth Century was, she said, "Ah, yes who the *hell*, indeed," and went on to explain that during the Crash, the woman's husband had announced he was leaving her, and she picked up both their children and hurled them off the roof of their skyscraper apartment building, for which she had spent all of three weeks in an asylum.

Marie and Willard also had two large dogs, a white one and a black one. Both were incredibly vicious. People used to wrap newspaper around their legs inside their trousers before they went over to visit at the penthouse, because the dogs would slink among the Victorian furniture, prowling, looking for a leg to gnaw. Marie loved them dearly, though, and they had to be put up with.

To go to Marie's and Willard's apartment was to encounter a test of the extremes of human emotion. Every visit was punctuated by a series of their quarrels which sometimes could get quite brutal.

Willard would bring his boys up to the penthouse — an endless stream of young men — and Marie would come to know all of them. It was to be Marie's way, for the rest of her life, to remain friends with Willard's lovers, and her friendship often long outlasted Willard's sexual relationship with them. She explained to me once that she did this in order to protect Willard, if he ever needed it (as he probably sometimes did, in the then dangerous world of New York City gay pick-up life). But I also supposed, then as now, that by befriending Willard's lovers she could remain closer to Willard.

Yet, Marie and Willard had their own bed, over which hung one of Marie's sand paintings, with an actual rattlesnake skin implanted in it, which she had titled "The Garden of Eden." The painting had a kind of magical connotation for Marie, because it constantly dripped water, making literal pools on and around the bed. Some of the magic was eventually taken away when a scientist friend of Marie's explained how the sand absorbed moisture from the air, which would then condense on the snakeskin and dribble down. But it remained a witty symbol for her.

In an interview with P. Adams Sitney in his *Filmwise* magazine, Marie said of her getting into film: "There is no why for my making films. I just liked the twitters of the machine, and since it was an extension of painting for me, I tried and I loved it." She had come by a camera when her friend Francis Lee went into the army. Francis Lee was a painter, but also had made a beautiful little film, "Le Bijou." Just before he left for the army, he put his camera into a hock shop and "bequeathed" the pawn ticket to Marie, who zipped over to the pawn shop and bought it out of hock. Her first work with this camera was in the making of one of Willard's films, "Geography of the Body," in 1943, which she helped to photograph. It was composed of extreme close-ups of the nude male body, images that were "set" to a poem by Willard and Marie's good friend the poet George Barker. Marie had gone out and bought a dime-store magnifying glass, which she taped to the camera lens, and with this crude equipment photographed most of "Geography of the Body." But this was Willard's film, not Marie's. Then, less than two years later, in 1945, she took the same camera and went into the studio of the sculptor Isamu Noguchi and cut loose on her own.

At this point, immediately after World War II, the West was only just beginning to recognize the art of Japan, but with great reservation. Marie had no such reservations. She had met Noguchi through her different friends in the art world, and had been working on something else for him, and, as she says in the *Filmwise* interview, "while I was experimenting around I had the advantage of looking around Isamu's studio with a clear, unobstructed eye. I asked if I might come in and shoot around, and he said yes. . . . And when he saw that footage, he was entertained and delighted. So was I. It was fun. All art should be fun in a sense and give one a kick."

So she barreled into Noguchi's studio with as big a noise as possible and as expansive a swinging of the camera, which must have practically disappeared in the enclosure of her large, cupped hands, just as Noguchi's sculptures probably seemed quite fragile as she danced among them, turning them this way and that on film. The result was "Visual Variations on Noguchi," with music by her good friend the composer Lucia Dlugoszewski. Marie once told me that, essentially, "Noguchi" was an attempt to capture "the flying spirit of movement within these solid objects." She wanted to get across "how they made me feel." This is one of the first films that took full advantage of the enormous freedom of the hand-held camera. In the history of cinema up to that time, Marie's was the most free-floating hand-held camera short of newsreel catastrophe shots; and "Visual Variations on Noguchi" liberated a lot of independent filmmakers from the idea that had been so powerful up to then, that we have to imitate the Hollywood dolly shot, without dollies — that the smooth pan and dolly was the only acceptable thing. Marie's free, swinging, swooping hand-held pans changed all that, for me and for the whole independent filmmaking world.

It was quite common, when this film was first shown, however, for at least one or two people to run screaming from the room — in terror, really, at the incredible energy of it, which we can still feel in all her work and, I'm sure, people always will be able to feel. This was also women's liberation — this was Marie, then, having her life through the art of the film. Marie, however, would say that I am being too heavy. I can hear her saying, "Women's lib, my dear? Really! It's women's luv!" Always, her wit was sharp and ready. I remember that I used to come out with things like, "Ah, Marie, this film's a miracle!" And she would eye me and say, "No, my dear, we're not walking on water this season."

One of her works, "Hurry! Hurry!" (released in 1957), puts "wit's end" on a whole new plane. The film had its genesis when a man, a scientist who ran a little film society in Wilmington, Delaware, came to see Willard and Marie. The film society was comprised of about seven or eight scientists who rented films by independent filmmakers. They had accumulated a certain purse of perhaps a hundred dollars and wanted to give it to a worthy film artist. They had decided to give it to Willard for his film "Geography of the Body." So this man was sent with the prize money to New York where he looked up Willard and Marie in their penthouse apartment. He was a little, bald-headed, shy man – I happened to be there when he arrived. They were thrilled and offered to show him some more films. He liked Marie's work so much, and was so confident that the other members of his film society would be as charmed by them, that he asked if there was anything he could do for her.

Now, during their conversation, it had come out that he was something of a photographer himself – and that he had taken microscopically magnified film of different cells and bacteria. His field, he had told Marie, was streptococcus – which later occasioned endless puns from Willard – and he had taken a lot of film footage of streptococci. So, when he asked if he could do anything for her benefit, she said, "Well, my dear, I don't know what I'd do with throat germs, but do you suppose you could get me some spermatozoa?"

He sent her some magnified spermatozoa images, out of which she made "Hurry! Hurry!," which of all her work she always referred to as her own favorite. It can be interpreted, on one level, as a portrait of Willard's life – the tragedy of Willard running from one gay bar to another trying to find a progenitive life for himself; and, like the spermatozoa, gradually dying out for lack of an egg. When, in his interview with Marie, P. Adams Sitney asked why she had once referred to this film as her saddest, she said, "Mighty sad when the sperm only seeks the sperm because it cannot find an egg – and then what? It collapses in death. . . . And see that film to see what death is really like, at the beginning — we know the fanfare, and at the end of life — what resignation. Oh, but get that beginning and the hopeless resignation to collapse. Wow!"

This is one of those exciting films which can exist on many levels. Marie made "Hurry! Hurry!" using the microscopy footage and footage of images of flames, an "A" roll and a "B" roll, one superimposed on the other. Most of the splices in this work — and here's a nice grubbiness of the day, being able to see the splices — are made to alter the quality of the flame, which makes a variety of rhythms, some of them very smooth as slower rhythm, others a heated rhythm. It is the flame's rhythms and their variety — achieved by Marie's keen splicing — which gives the film its life. Against this flame image, then, are the images of the spermatazoa and their rhythms, which involved more detailed splicing.

The little spermatozoon that is "Willard" can also be seen as a note of music, an eighth-note, say. Wherever this little eighth-note pauses or whirls around, she would make the cut to place it rhythmically in the following scene. That is, if the next scene is a cluster of spermatozoa, then the lone spermatozoon from the preceding scene is — bang! just like that — in its place, through what is called the plastic cut. It's here, alone, moving in a particular rhythm, and in the next scene we see a cluster of spermatozoa with one carrying the same rhythm as was in the previous scene. The story is thereby carried on — or the melody, the rhythm.

But the major cuts were made to alter the quality of the flame which provides the "bass" rhythm as well as repeated visual shape — or "bass vision." The "themes and variations" of the spermatazoa images play against the "bass" of the flame images, making this an almost perfect Baroque work of art.

The flame pulses, but obviously never *exactly* repeating either its rhythms or its shapes; and in this regard "Hurry! Hurry!" is kindred to an essential aesthetic of Gertrude Stein: Marie often seems to be repetetive but, like Stein, she never is. Marie's epic masterpiece, in this respect as well as several others, is "Go! Go! Go!" (1963). Here, the people of the city of New York seem locked into repetetive movements by the grids of the streets and the pulse of the traffic; by the ritualistic antics of graduation ceremonies or muscle-men exhibits (photographed, no doubt, to tease Willard); and by their own habits such as are depicted in the three shots of Willard getting up from his typewriter to stare at the Manhattan skyline, each time throwing his hands into the air ecstatically before pouncing on the typewriter once more. But Marie's hand-held camera prevents any and every sense of repetition one might begin feeling; so that the little "city symphony" that is "Go! Go! Go!" manages to show the entire trappings of the metropolis without the consequent despair of either Ruttmann's "Berlin" or that which prevails in the more recent "Koyannisqatsi" whose makers got their technique from Marie's work but missed her spirit altogether.

What Marie essentially "mothered" into film was cinematic collage. As a painter in the collage tradition she embedded into thick paint both hard and soft objects. She also mixed the paint with various textures, such as sand, and "wove" objects through her paint and across the surfaces of her canvasses. When she came to film, then, she looked at it first of all as a "thread" of many shades and colors to be woven or "spun out" into related patterns. She would hold the strips of film in her hand very much as she would strands of beads to be put into a collage painting. She would hang the film strips on clothespins and, after much meditation and often without running them through a viewer at all, would cut them together. Finally, of course, she would view the film over the projector because, as she once pointed out to me, "You cannot judge back-and-forth movements very well looking at the film strip — unless they are very fast in-and-out movements."

Often, she under-cranked her camera to increase speed of depth movement. But primarily, at least in her early films, she concentrated on pans and tilts of the camera in relationship to objects on a plane with the surface of the film, often employing flats, such as Dwight Ripley's paintings, with objects animated across their surface, as in her 1959 film, "Dwightiana"; or extreme close-up photography to flatten the plane as in "Geography of the Body" and "Glimpse of the Garden"; or, as in "Hurry! Hurry!," microscopy. Marie was especially fond, in her later work, of photographing lights; but she almost always avoided halos and lens refractions: her lights were sharp-focused, correctly exposed flat light cut-outs, as those in "Moonplay," or hard calligraphic streaks, as in the end of her last film, "Lights."

Marie was also a cinematic poet in the sense that she made a translation of poetic possibilities into the language of cinema. She was deeply involved with poetry to the extent, for example, that she only read English poetry knowing full well that poetry does not translate from one written language to another – "and, my dear," she would say, "as there is more than enough English poetry to read in a lifetime, why bother with attempts at translations from other languages?"

Thus, when I say that she translated poetry into cinema, I mean that she had to invent a cinematic corollary, and one which would not diminish the art of language with some cheap pictorialization of verbal meanings. Her tactic was to take notice of what the two media, poetry and film, share – that they are continuity arts very dependent on rhythm – and work with that. Marie had a marvelous eye for rhythmic detail, the fastest mind's eye of cinema in her time, and could capture metaphorical relationships in most of her photography and hold them visually taut along a strand of film. Then she would structure the pattern "stanzas" of these strands in the editing of the strips. Two of the best examples of this are in her "Bagatelle for Willard Maas" (1961), which intercuts scenes of Versailles with images in their home; and "Go! Go! Go!," in which she gracefully tackles the complexities of New York City and the varieties of public ceremony and private "home-movie" living. But it is in the privacy of her art – akin to the hidden meanings turned metaphorical in Emily Dickinson's works – where we find the poet Marie Menken.

Marie achieved a mastery of rhythm which very few have matched and, I think, none have surpassed in the history of film. If you approach her works with the same expectation as you would bring to a piece of poetry or music, you get the most from them. The visual rhythms cohere with each other and in relationship to the soundtracks, some of which were created by Teiji Ito, Maya Deren's last husband.

Marie called on Teiji to create soundtracks for "Hurry! Hurry!," "Bagatelle for Willard Maas" and "Dwightiana," among others. I remember how once she said, with her usual exuberance and not without some vindictiveness, "Well, my dear, one good thing about having outlived Maya – *I* now have Teiji." Still, she had a great deal of respect for Maya Deren as a filmmaker and Maya respected Marie as a painter – although Maya, like Willard, failed to recognize Marie as the great filmmaker she was, perhaps in Maya's case at least, because Marie's films were so free from drama, so much more intrinsically filmic.

Although she used soundtracks, Marie's films stand on their own as great visual works. The use of sound in film has often been criticized – and I am one of those critics – as a gimmick, a crutch that helps the film along when the visuals fall apart, or as a distraction. But Marie never added soundtracks to make up for a lack of visual excitement. She explained it best to P. Adams Sitney: "If visual excitement is lacking, I have failed. Music or sound is added for kicks and nothing else. To prove this, run off any of my films without sound and you will get the jolts and rhythms of the visual chances, silent as they are, to a capacity of feeling."

Marie's 1957 "Glimpse of the Garden" is another of her films which sprang directly from her particular situation. It was shot in the garden of Dwight Ripley, an old boyfriend of Willard's and a wealthy man. Dwight was an alcoholic who was forever having rich people's troubles – which are absolutely incurable – and he had become very dependent on Marie. She came to love him deeply, long after Willard was through with him, and they were great friends. Dwight was a painter and, as well, was passionately involved with gardening. Through his fortune, he was able to import rare plants and spend his considerable leisure cultivating a beautiful, exotic garden.

Marie enters Dwight's garden very much in the spirit with which she had entered Noguchi's studio, but also with the impulses that she put into "Hurry! Hurry!" She is, along the line of the petals in Dwight's garden, telling a tale. "Glimpse of the Garden" is one of the toughest of Marie's works. If you aren't watching for rhythm, you might as well stay in the lobby with your cigarette, because rhythm and tone used in an intensified musical way is the whole experience of the film. If you want a movie about flowers, find something in Disney's nature series. Marie's film really works Dwight Ripley's garden of rare and unique flowers. What she does with them is to turn them more completely into film than I think flowers have been, before or since.

Portraiture was another filmic frontier that Marie pioneered. Her "Dwightiana," "Arabesque for Kenneth Anger" and "Bagatelle for Willard Maas" arrived at that very instant when the only concept of portraiture there then was in film – and still is, too much – was in terms of "taking a picture"; which is to say with very little giving into it, certainly not the sort of investment that had made oil portraiture great. There had also always been the sense that a portrait had to demonstrate the distinguishing features of a face, but this could not be the business of film as it could be with oil painting. Marie solved that dilemma. As she put it in her interview with Sitney, "I have a feeling about these people and somehow created, cinematically speaking, what moves them or what has moved me, having what I thought was an insight into their own creative work. A general audience can be reached if I am a good communicant, and if not, it is my loss. . . . I might say that I was quite personal in my approach [to the portrait films], an extravagance for those who had a true feeling in their creative work."

Marie made portraits of her subjects by photographing the things that these people would love, or did love, and she did so in ways which, being at her desperate wit's end, betray her thoughts of their character — always with humor. "I want to impart hilarity, joyousness," she said to Sitney, "expansion of life with an uncontrollable mirth."

People have often remarked that she was getting back at Willard with "Bagatelle." But that feeling is really the result of the soundtrack — Teiji Ito's heavy-handed annoyance with Willard. Teiji could hardly be regarded as a sympathizer of Willard's; in fact, he was turned off completely by the extravagance of Willard's gayness. His annoyance with Willard came through in the music he did for "Bagatelle," and that created an imbalance in the film in comparison to Marie's images. For all that Marie understood Willard — and hated him at the same time, and was the butt of his abuse and beatings — for all that, she never blamed him, at least not publicly, over her life being so restricted as a consequence of his circumstances. Others — including Teiji — did, but she did not believe it was Willard's fault that she loved a man who loved other men, or that he had come to discover the nature of his sexuality after he had married her. Marie never approved of Teiji's almost strident anti-gay attitude. It was so much her greatness, really, that she accommodated Willard and loved him and his lovers. And I think that a close viewing of any of her films would reveal the authenticity of her feelings toward homosexuality in general and her gay friends in particular. "There is love and it is everywhere," she said to Sitney. "There is no loss, except for those who do not love — and it is their own loss."

Marie was shy. She was always the hidden one, and she always hid her camera behind Willard as much as possible until finally she was discovered as the consequence of the pressures of her friends — which only got her Willard's rages and beatings.

Still, she loved Willard. When she went to Versailles, to shoot footage for "Bagatelle," another filmmaker friend and I accompanied her. I remember her joy at finding images that would appeal to Willard. Imagine this large Lithuanian woman hurling herself into the air with her little, obviously amateur camera in hand, on the golden gates of Versailles. Or, faced with that immense landscape pruned to an absolute T, with a ten-mile view of a lake cut into the shape of a key, exclaiming, "Oooooh! Willard would *love* this!" And she began photographing the fountains going off all over the place, because Willard *would* — and *did* — love it.

Willard was always "the artist," the coddled one. He was most often out of a job — he was always "too sensitive" to hold one down. So it was Marie who worked, bringing home the money. For all of their married life she worked for Time-Life; and every evening, five and sometimes six days a week, Marie trudged up to the Time-Life Building for the night shift, to pick up all the overnight cables from whatever state or country she was handling that night, and held that job for thirty years. She would come home at two or three o'clock in the morning and drink herself into sleep. Gradually, the drinking began to encroach into the afternoon, until, finally, she was drunk most of the time when she wasn't making a film or at her job at Time-Life.

Marie loved making films, but not many people in the film art world of her time thought of her as a serious filmmaker. Marie knew perfectly well who and what she was, but her way of dealing with the inattention was to treat her own works more lightly than they should have been treated; in fact, she never showed much interest in her finished works as works of art to be preserved. She never thought of making a print, but ran the original film on crappy old projectors and thereby destroyed some of them over repeated showings. The whole deterioration process was aggravated by the fact that she (and Willard, and many other independent filmmakers of the time) used already outdated film. Marie would get bits and pieces of film that could be begged from labs — often war surplus film that had been manufactured to be used in bomber planes during the war. It was Willard who kept insisting that she make prints of certain films he liked, and insisting so vehemently, that finally she would send them off to the lab.

This is not to say that Willard had become, finally, an ardent supporter of Marie's work. The fact is that he was always putting her down. He would put her down in that way men do with women: After a long evening of viewing his films, when everyone was tired and ready to leave, he would say, "Oh, Marie's films are *sooooo* wonderful — you *also* have to see one of her little productions." He never took her film work seriously; he never wanted anyone else to, either. But that wasn't what they fought about — until later, when she became famous and was recognized as an absolute visual poet, and his films were falling out of favor. Then the awful truth came home to roost. After ten or fifteen years of abusing Marie's films and laughing them off — saying, "Oh, yes, and Marie also plays around with the camera" — he suddenly found himself influenced by Marie's camera.

Willard Maas's own "The Silver Flotation of Andy Warhol" harked back, twenty years later, to Marie's Noguchi film, which Willard had passed off as a silly woman's adventure. Now he knew that, technically, she was tops on him with the camera, and, in fact, in his soul he must have known that she was, clearly, the genuine artist all the time.

Marie avoided posing as "the artiste" in her lifetime, with the result that she could *be* an artist. Willard had adopted the affectations of "the artiste" to such an extent that he could no longer free himself of his persona and create an art of his own.

Marie's drinking finally killed her. She died in 1970 when she was in her late fifties. Four days later, Willard, who had been deteriorating under drugs, also died. It was probably the only romantic thing he ever did in his relationship with Marie Menken.

Photo: Mike Chikiris

Sidney Peterson

I first met Sidney Peterson in New York at the home of Amos Vogel where he was showing "Mr. Frenhofer and the Minotaur," which I think is his greatest work. He had this smile that was like those parted curtains that drape themselves into big puffs above the drawstring and then little puffs underneath. His face is like a band-box stage with a pair of sharp intellectual lips sitting in the center of it. Oh, I wouldn't say a dry narrow mouth, but in that direction — sharp, clean. When he spoke, he spoke rapidly and to the point. I remember also that when he laughed, he had laugh wrinkles not only at the sides of his eyes, but down through the bags under his eyes — which I had never seen before and haven't seen since on any other face.

Sidney was always smiling, the lower half of his face rather symmetrically parted, like a curtain, but from the forehead up his features were almost asymmetrical, as though the top of his head, the brain, etc., were fighting it out from right to left. For instance, his hairline was receding unevenly. His two vertical frown lines were aimed diagonally across toward his nose, and his brow was furrowed. Beneath this struggle, his eyes, nose, lips seemed always determined to maintain the mask of wit.

He was the kind of man who was both shy and very sophisticated. He would stand up very shyly to shake your hand and smile, almost obsequiously, and then he would sit there and stare at you archly, cross his legs and begin. I think this is a quality that is felt in all of Sidney's work. He had a tremendous shyness. You could almost see him as the little boy called "Sidney" (who did not look too different from the boy in his film "The Potted Psalm"), cursed as are all boys named Sidney, who was bookish and somewhat shunned by his fellow students, and who in maturity developed a tremendous power of intellect.

A bit on Peterson's background. This is from the biographical notes written for his novel, *The Fly in the Pigment*:

> Sidney Peterson was born in 1912 in Oakland, California. He is widely traveled and . . . widely educated. He started out to become a sculptor, then went to sea for several years, changed his mind again and studied medicine at the University of California for three years, after which he went to work for a newspaper. He next became a draftsman for a naval architect but left this in order to make a movie with James Broughton. Meanwhile he was writing on various topics, such as the religious life of a lunatic (unpublished), psychoanalytic aspects of English literature, and the visual prospect of London. He founded a film company in Seattle, spent two years with the Museum of Modern Art as a television director and writer, founded Workshop 20, and ultimately went to Hollywood where he wrote cartoon scenarios for UPA and Walt Disney. . . . From Hollywood he moved to San Francisco where he now lives. . . .

Sidney Peterson was known to me years before I met him; but our paths had crossed, beginning at the California School of Fine Arts (now, the San Francisco Art Institute), where he had taught from about 1945 until shortly before I arrived there in 1951. I will have to describe the school to you a little bit. All those who have ever been there, or know the San Francisco area, refer to it as "800 Chestnut Street." Going down the hill toward it, with the vision of Alcatraz Island dead ahead, you make a right onto Chestnut and there is a building of old missionary type architecture. It had cracked walls and peeling paint — the usual art school nonsense, but it did have a lovely little garden in an enclosed courtyard out back.

The California School of Fine Arts was certainly one of the great art schools of America at the time. Clyfford Still was teaching there, Hassel Smith, Richard Diebenkorn, Ansel Adams, Minor White and, of course, Sidney Peterson. It was quite a congregation of people. We are talking about 1945 to the early fifties. Many GIs had enrolled under the GI Bill; many of them had faced death and had seen things on battlefields almost beyond our imagination; and they had come back determined to gain something. That was the spirit that prevailed all over the country. You had your normal high school graduates coming into college at this time, but you also had these fiercely dedicated men, hardened by war and informed by the wisdom, not only of several more years, but of intensive and suffering years. And they were determined to make something of the school.

This atmosphere made even the most humdrum colleges blossom. If you then had teachers of any worth – as was the case at the California School of Fine Arts – you created in young people such as myself a feeling that America was absolutely going to have to have a renaissance. Why it didn't was simply that after several years these GIs finished whatever schooling they had to finish – or they dropped out, or went crazy – and the Beatnik movement began. You then had only high school graduates, very coddled students for the most part, and it all went back to "normal," where it has been ever since.

Peterson was one who thrived on teaching these GIs. I would say that the major body of his work was made not only at this school, but using for the most part these young students and these disturbed GIs to create a series of masterpieces.

Keep in mind that around Sidney were Ansel Adams, with his extremely beautiful, fussy sense of "gray-scale" printing; Minor White, who would be the younger man under Adams, going on to develop his ideas in his own particular genius, and those great painters I have mentioned, including Clyfford Still. Clyfford Still used to teach his classes by telling his students that they were there, the materials were there, and they were expected to paint. If they could not paint at the school, then they could go home and paint, and if they could not paint in either place, then they should drop the course. If they had any questions serious enough to bother him with, then he would go out to coffee with them. Of course, most of the exciting conversations took place in the coffee room; it became a tradition, and you would see the model and everyone sitting around in the coffee room discussing art. This was the sort of atmosphere of the school. Everyone taught according to his own methods.

Then it all ended, when something occurred which tends to occur over and over again in American art schools. The semester previous to my arrival there, a new director had come in and found what he considered to be a reign of total anarchy. He began instituting changes, demanding that the faculty all start using textbooks, giving tests and so forth. So about thirty-five teachers walked out in a big explosion of anger in one day. I do not know for sure if Sidney Peterson was among those who walked out, but knowing his character as I do, I would think he just coincidentally left at the same time.

So there was no Sidney Peterson at 800 Chestnut Street when I arrived. (There was instead a man who was so ill-equipped to teach film, that after enduring three weeks of his fussing with the splicer I ran off with the camera and learned how to load it myself, and began doing work on my own.) But I did begin seeing Peterson's work then. Before he began teaching, he had already made one film, with James Broughton, called "The Potted Psalm."

A little of how it fell out that these two men happened to get together: They met at the end of the war, through a mutual friend, and at first tried collaborating on a play. In time, the play was supplanted by "The Potted Psalm." This unlikely collaboration could, and did, happen in that casual time of San Francisco when artists dropped in on each other and met at parties, in the street, in the grocery store. This was the San Francisco of 1945-46. There was no smog and very little industrial development. The old houses were still there, and beautifully so. It was a lovely city to take a walk in, and it was common for people to walk a lot and drop in on each other. It was quite ordinary for someone to drop in while a painter was working. You would have a cup of coffee and chat a while, and the guest would move on. It was a very loose city then, a very familiar city, and while one cannot claim that San Francisco was an art colony in 1945, you can claim that it has continually had a viable kind of art colonialism going on within it. In those days, whole neighborhoods in the city behaved very much as 800 Chestnut Street did.

Let me tell you what San Francisco did *not* have: It did not have a vested interest in European art, like New York City had (and still has, to its aesthetic damnation). And then as now, there was utter hopelessness in terms of any market for art in San Francisco. No artist could make even a half-assed living, not even as a teacher of art at that time, and this meant that no one was fighting with anyone, jockeying for positions with the galleries or notice from some critic on *The New York Times*. Oh, little galleries opened here and there, and friends of the artist, his mother, his girlfriend and her friends came to see his work, but that was about it.

Now, it should be stated as simple fact that Peterson and Broughton did not get along together making "The Potted Psalm." They started to make the movie. Each had ideas of his own. They disagreed, and the film was finished with difficulty. But even though Broughton was unhappy with the relationship in making the film, he was nonetheless very excited when it was finished, and he came to the world premiere.

"The Potted Psalm" is, I think, one of the least seductive films I have ever seen, and that is rather a triumph that Peterson stumbled into, although it is intrinsic to his work to be very flat with his wit, to be very clear and always to reveal his techniques and disguises. One of the reasons people often get so infuriated with this film is its lack of seduction. By seduction, I mean anything that leads you on. In the history of film, it certainly tends to be a technique which is the ambition of Hollywood. Any movie made in Hollywood, or for TV, is designed essentially to lead the viewer on, to suck the viewer into the screen. Works of art in film also utilize seduction to bring the viewer to a certain position. I mean a very attractive or beautiful image, or a very rhythmic or jazzy combination of images which will pull any person to attention. But if it is a work of art, as I understand it, this "seduction" must not lead you on but stop right at the image so that you are left hanging, not quite in your chair but somewhere between the chair and the screen – whereas Hollywood-type titillating seduction leaves you "on the edge of your seat."

But it is the lack of seduction and the ambiguity of viewpoint that make this film almost a work of art. In fact, I think I would vote for it as art. It is at least an incredibly unique example of art that has little seduction and complete ambiguity. As I watch this film year after year, Peterson's continuous ambiguity – which irritated me at first so that I tended to reject it – became, to me, one of the intrinsic values of "The Potted Psalm." I began to ask, "How does he make it work?"

You have no viewpoint in this film. You have a protagonist, but you do not know whether you are seeing from his viewpoint or from the viewpoint of someone else looking at him; or whether he is a she at the end, when the protagonist is running away in a skirt, but running like a man. Either the protagonist is "The Headless One" in the film, or the headless figure is the object of his desire. For instance, when "The Headless One" is pouring the drinks down, holding the girl – is that a metaphor for "the hero"? Is it in fact "the hero"? Is it another person? Are you seeing this from "The Headless One's" viewpoint . . . or from the camera's viewpoint? Or does the film have a first-person viewpoint? You see the glass being raised up to the lens of the camera, the cigarette being raised up and smoke coming out, so that the camera is looking, the young man is looking, people are looking at him. He is or is not a metaphor; he is a he or a she, or she is, or is she?

This is the wonderful thing that is going on in the film; and after I studied "The Potted Psalm" a little further, I began to see that there is an intrinsic order to this ambiguity. It did not occur haphazardly, as one might first think. This is a very complicated work, because Sidney is certainly not going to be easily ambiguous, and he is not going to be easily formal, either, as long as he has gone to all this trouble. But there actually is a very formal order, a simple story, in fact; and a specific plot runs through the film.

Some people may consider Peterson's work – and this film in particular – to be naive. But in fact the manner of Peterson's films is anything but naive. The manner is "studied ambiguity," which is one of the most difficult things to accomplish in art. It is like trying to accomplish "articulate chaos." The naivete of "The Potted Psalm" is the feeling of grubbiness of the photography, the dirty puns, the objects that don't quite work in any seductive sense in relationship to each other; the masks, the jokes, the kind of brutal jocularity about mothers.

The film starts with the mother's grave: it is laid on Mother's grave in the beginning. Taking off from Mother's grave it goes to a woman who runs like a man, or a man in drag. In the meantime, the headless protagonist (or aspect of the protagonist) takes to "art." He is in a temple with his foot on a kind of impossible antique chair, playing an accordian. The joke there is that the man *should* be playinga flute, not an accordian, not with his booted foot on an antique chair. It is an incredible metaphor for "the American Youth" trying to work his way into art.

There is another way in which "The Potted Psalm" is unseductive and frustrates people. Many viewers feel that this boy, "the hero," can't act, that the women in the film can't act. And there are specific mannerisms which many find annoying: the boy makes a broad rhetorical gesture — and people say that this is not what we are used to from drama films; this certainly is not reality — people don't gesture like that. The truth of the matter is that they do. I imagine that these shell-shocked GIs in Peterson's class were people gesturing like that rather often. In fact, if you walk down the street and look at what people are doing, you'll see that "The Potted Psalm" *could* even be regarded as a realistic drama of human behavior. Actually, though, it isn't that, either. It is very studied; and what Sidney does that is so brave, so courageous in his work is to state this fact of "study" also: Peterson did have one mental foot in European thought.

Perhaps I should have said, earlier, that San Francisco did have a little bit of a toe, at least, in Europe; and Sidney, as so many people living in California at that time, did have his big toe in surrealism. Take Nathanael West as an excellent example of this in literature. He was called an "American surrealist," but actually he does not fit within the surrealist movement at all. West demonstrates what happens to surrealism when it hits the United States. Again, with Sidney, you see what happens to surrealism in film in the United States. Look at the famous "Andalusian Dog," by Buñuel and Dali; and then look at "The Potted Psalm." "The Potted Psalm" is a much more honest film and a much more meaningful film, to me at least, than the "Andalusian Dog." Bunuel and Dali filled that film with seduction and all the bric-a-brac of European seductive art. The moment the drama starts dragging with loose form, ants come out of a hole in a hand, photographed in such a composed way that they might be on the ceiling of the Sistine Chapel. "The Andalusian Dog" is extremely seductive, whereas in Sidney's films everything is alive, as it is in America.

In "The Potted Psalm" Sidney Peterson says nothing on the soundtrack; however, we do have some of his films that do use the soundtrack to say something. Everything is awry with Peterson. If you use your little guide book of Sigmund Freud to try to interpret

"The Potted Psalm" or another of his films, say, "The Petrified Dog," you will get nowhere. If anyone told Sigmund Freud that they ran their hand down a woman's leg and came upon a spiral table leg, he would interpret it, but it would not be an interpretation of what Sidney Peterson does in his film. What I am getting at is that Sidney Peterson is beyond all interpretation.

Sidney made a comment on this, which should also settle the question of the ambiguity in his films: "These images are meant to play, not on our rational sense, but on the infinite universe of ambiguity that is within us." Now, mind, this sounds at first like Dali and Bunuel. They published a statement saying that when they made "The Andalusian Dog" they took only pictures of things that they had no rational explanation for. That sounds very close to Peterson's statement, but the difference in the way he puts it is crucial. It is as crucial as the difference between Confucius and Christ. Confucius, who came earlier, said, "Do not do unto your neighbors that which you would not have them do unto you." Christ said, "Do unto your neighbor as you would have him do unto you." There is a hell of a difference there, at least as much difference as between the European surrealism of Dali and Buñuel and Peterson's "The Potted Psalm." Peterson's film is a positive work. For all that it looks grubby and disturbing, it is extremely positive and forthright.

The world premiere showing of "The Potted Psalm" took place at the San Francisco Museum of Art as part of the Art in Cinema series, which was being run by Frank Stauffacher. Now, Frank Stauffacher was one of those beautiful and exciting people who loved films as much as any man on earth. He was also a filmmaker, with a number of fine films to his credit; one of them, "Sausalito," is a masterpiece in my opinion. Stauffacher convinced the museum to permit him to run an Art in Cinema series, and at that time this was the only series like it in any museum west of New York. When Stauffacher gave "The Potted Psalm" its premiere showing, people howled and were outraged. It created quite a disturbance. Of course, there is no point in creating such public outrage over art in America. When people riot over art they are just imitating turn-of-the century-France. We don't have any time for that here; there are more important things to riot about. There is just no point in people booing and hissing and throttling each other over something that is on the screen.

In 1948, a year after "The Potted Psalm" was made, Peterson made "The Petrified Dog." One of the central metaphors in this film is Art – the making of it, the damaging of it. Certainly, the film can be seen on this simple level alone. To a child it certainly seems very strange (and I know of no better image of it that has ever been created) that a man should have a frame and paint what is all around, but paint it onto the frame.

It takes all of any grown man's intellect to recognize child wisdom, which operates very greatly in this film. Take, for instance, this wonderful scene – the view of the painter trying to get acceptance of his painting; and his friend, the critic, standing there going on and on about it, as the painter's wife has done; and then the painter reaches into his pocket and offers his friend the critic a cup of water, as any painter would offer his work, just as simply as, "If you are thirsty, would you like a drink of water?" In this scene we know immediately that the critic's refusal of the cup of water is one of the cruelest, meanest things on earth.

The metaphor is made quite clearly; but in addition, as with all Sidney's metaphors, it grows out of an earlier metaphor of the man reaching into his pocket to pull out what we presume to be a weapon to defend himself, but he could never get that weapon out of his pocket. And that creates another metaphor, of a little boy playing with his penis in his pocket. So you see, there is a constantly growing series of metaphors in this work, springing from a single trunk, which you might call a view of putrefaction through the eyes of the little girl in the film. Her eyes are quite distinctly different from those of the boy in "The Potted Psalm," but you might say that these two works go together beautifully in that they are a double work — facing pages of each other, one male, one female.

Sidney would be aware, of course, that a girl would have to come to the sense of the ambiguity of the world in terms of sex much earlier than the boy of "The Potted Psalm" would. Sidney was also the man who could deal with this child-sight of "The Petrified Dog" and assume a woman's viewpoint. There are very few male artists who are successful at this. D.H. Lawrence is known for his ability to write almost as though he were a woman, and not in the sense of being homosexual, but quite the opposite. Lawrence actually assumes the views of the woman and presents them faithfully in both poetry and novels. Peterson also possessed that quality, that ability.

To get another look at Sidney Peterson, it would be appropriate also to read his novel, *The Fly in the Pigment*, published by Angel Island Publishers. It is a bit difficult to find, but I have seen it in a few bookstores, so you might be able to find a copy. The story is very simple, as are all of Sidney's stories. A fly in a painting that is hanging in the Louvre — a painted fly — takes off, leaves the painting. The following excerpt begins as a parody of the speech of a professor, Dr. Fontainas, and parts of it are very close to the kind of talk I normally heard from Sidney:

> "Mesdames et Messieurs, most serious historians will, I think, agree that the Muse of History is not Clio but Mother Goose. Yes. Mother Goose. A fly disappears from a painting. At once we are back in the age of fables. A carved dog starts running. A widow has a child by a clay statue of her husband, who has been quite incapable of producing offspring. A horse of a particular color turns out to be the work of a certain artist, other horses are so charged with vitality that they gallop right out of the picture and dragons soar through ceilings after leaving the walls on which they have been painted. The artist wanders off into the landscape he has created and disappears forever. . . ."

Let me give you a sense of his conversation. Most of Sidney's writing is, I think, too thick and dense to reflect his conversation. But there is another passage from *The Fly in the Pigment* that comes close:

> Lice and fleas have won more battles than all the generals in history. The generals are well aware of this fact. They know they can't fight a big modern war without an adequate insecticide. In 1914 they had pyrethrum. With tremendous effort they managed to hold the western front but in the east lice were completely successful. It is estimated that from 1917 to 1921 there were more than 15 million cases of louse-borne typhus in the territories controlled by the Soviet Republic.

Perhaps you have known people who will come up with statements such as, "In 1938 there were 232,000 miles of telegraph wires in Mozambique." There are people with that kind of information, and Sidney is definitely one of them. He would give you these statements. I used to think that he was totally pulling my leg – that he was making these things up. But I began to realize that his facts were accurate. And that is a quality which is also important in his films.

A conversation with Sidney which sticks in my mind occurred when I quoted to him the fact that Gertrude Stein said that we cannot communicate. That statement always lies very heavily on my mind. I almost use it as a prayer bead. Gertrude Stein was asked, "Why is it that preachers, teachers, orators, politicians, etc. all die mentally before they are 35 years of age?" She answered – and again I am paraphrasing – "Because they begin to believe that they can communicate." Well, I was feeling that I had been on too many lecture tours, and I was kind of moping, and I quoted this to Sidney. He said, "Oh, well, that's all right – you can just take whatever it is that people do when they talk and call that communication and forget it."

He had that kind of mind, that could completely see Gertrude Stein's viewpoint and say OK to it and contradict it in the same breath. He could never take dictum as final. He was interested in facts, not infinity.

In all conversation I had with him, he came on very flat with clear sensibility. I would come to him and say, "Oh, Sidney, God, it's awful – I can't make a living this year, and the government's done thus and so, and one of the film club's folded, and it's all hopeless, and I'm thinking of just building a big pile of my films and pouring gasoline over them and burning them publicly." And he would reply, "Now, that's something that hasn't been tried yet," and add, "We all keep hoping you'll make it." He would take my statement and would not treat it as absurd, but throw it back at me in a way that showed the absolute absurdity of it.

I never met Sidney when, in two or three brief sentences, he didn't give me things to brood upon, things that would shape my work for years to come. I suppose that altogether Sidney and I have met ten or twelve times, in such places as doughnut shops, at cocktail parties and, on two or three lovely occasions, in his apartment. His apartment is amazing. It is decorated with Kwakiutl masks, among other things. These masks are very disturbing, and I cannot properly describe the experience of sitting in their presence. On the surface, Peterson's apartment looks very normal – supernormal – but the minute you begin looking at the specific objects in it, you realize that it is as wild and incredible as his films.

Laughter is very important to him, too. If you want to get a great fix on Peterson's sense of humor, look up an article of his that appeared in *Film Culture Reader.* The subject is humor, and it is outrageously funny. He suggests that artists working with humor ought to use canned laughter to get the audience going, or hire laughter people. Laughter is very important to him because it counterbalances what otherwise would be extremely heavy metaphor. If you are not laughing with his films, they begin to lie heavily on the head – if not the heart.

His humor is there in his film "The Lead Shoes," as is his great sense of metaphor and his "studied ambiguity." The soundtrack of this film gives us two major themes: "Three black crows sat on a fence" and "Edward, my son . . . where did you get that blood on your hands?" Is it "black" crows or "old" crows? It is both, of course, because the melody is "three black sheep," and the reference (the main reference) is to the three Fates or three sisters or three witches and/or the whole kit-kaboodle of the White Goddess ("Mama Fate") turned "black" and "sitting on the fence" — like we say when we mean "being neutral." But the fence stands also for that one of insomnia which imaginary sheep are supposed to jump over. These sheep — turned to crows — sit on the fence: a torturous frieze, the moreso inasmuch as crows might fly. These are first crow-birds as well as "old crows" (as they are called later in the song), and we might even say "crow-bars" for opening up this film.

But leave it to Sidney to be always *literal*. "The Lead Shoes" documents the life of a diving suit which is no doubt literally weighted with lead in its shoes. The "mama" figure in the film takes the diving suit as her son — or is it her husband?, or her father? The voice on the soundtrack leads us to the assumption via screaming calls of "Edward . . . EDWARD," and "Mama" proceeds to dig up the suit magically (with the film running a backward take of her actually burying it), and she takes it/him home through the streets of San Francisco.

If the diving suit is her son Edward, she is burying it, if we are to believe the soundtrack. If the diving suit is her husband, then she is surely digging it up — digging up the father whom the old English ballad suggests Edward killed. If that suit is "Mama's" father, then what are we to think? As the "three black/old crows" theme suggests, "Mama" can be Matriarchy itself, which would make of that old suit Zeus (or, more literally, Neptune); or God the Father, Son and Holy Ghost all rolled into one.

Thus all these stories are unfolding one at a time throughout "The Lead Shoes." This is ambiguity at its best. It is an ambiguity which Peterson creates by way of exhaustive means. He exhausts all classical meanings intrinsic to the situation and thereby leaves the viewer at the mercy of the immediate imagery and language of the film itself. Every attempt at symbolic or historic understanding of "The Lead Shoes" is bound to destruct against the multiplicity of meanings, leaving the thoughtful viewer with scattered wits — though *not* at wit's end — which is also a consequence of the same technique Peterson employed in making "Mr. Frenhofer and the Minotaur."

It is vitally important for a full appreciation of "The Lead Shoes" to try to beat it at its own game — to try to follow its many levels of meaning clear through — because only these experiences of mental defeat really open the viewer to the film. Try as you will — and exactly as in a gambling casino — you cannot win, cannot wring a coherent set of meanings from the film. Sidney has stacked the deck masterfully! The means, or themes, of "The Lead Shoes" are deliberately edited at cross-purposes. No simple warp and woof here, but rather one of the most masterful frays of meaning ever created — thus, one of the greatest celebrations of Mystery I have ever experienced.

Take "the thigh bone connected to the . . ." say, the penis of Edward or Father/Whomever . . . "connected to the body and blood of our Lord Jesus Christ," in the scene where the bone is placed on the plate for the French poodle. The bone becomes bread, which is broken open, drips blood, cross-connecting itself to the Communion — bread and . . . blood? — flesh and . . . bone? — What?! And roar with laughter, finally — or with terror, if you prefer.

We have to realize that when we speak of Peterson's sense of comedy in film, we are up against all the "big guns" of intentional comedy — comedy that was made specifically to sell and to sell quickly and widely, and was designed to make people laugh. We are up against Chaplin, Keaton, Laurel and Hardy, and many others of that caliber. At the extreme opposite are Sidney Peterson's films made at the California School of Fine Arts. We cannot view them in the same context as the commercial films, but as art. That would be the whole point, and a point which I think would amuse Sidney very much.

Sidney's tendency was to be exceedingly thoughtful. He would work along the line of ideas, also taking the ideas of others, that is, whatever his students would suggest and act out for the camera. Someone would say, "Let's do this," and someone else would say, "I'll do this." Many of the resulting routines were based on classic comedy, on Chaplinesque and Keatonesque comedy sequences. For instance, the chiropractor sequence in "The Petrified Dog" has similarities to Chaplin in the chiropractor's hands in "The Cure." Various things were suggested to Peterson, and he took them and orchestrated them, so that is why it is sometimes a little difficult to follow story lines in his work.

When Peterson made his films, he made them for the sake of making them. Then they were shown in Art in Cinema; there was some publicity and word got around. After everyone had left college, Peterson went to New York City and took some prints of his films with him. The films were seen by Amos Vogel at Cinema 16 and were very much appreciated by him. Vogel immediately put them on the Cinema 16 program, and Peterson became known as a filmmaker. First the films were distributed by Cinema 16 and later, by Grove Press, which had bought out Cinema 16. So that is how it all happened.

At one point, I met Sidney in a doughnut shop in La Cienaga, in Los Angeles. At that time the Coronet Theater, run by Raymond Rohauer, was attempting to buy some of his films to show regularly. I was working at the Coronet, so we all went out for coffee. It was on that occasion that Sidney did something that has always been very important to me. He had seen some of my films, and when we went to the doughnut shop, he brought along his anamorphic lens which he had used for all distortion shots, and he gave it to me. It was a simple gift. It passed across the table. I took it and thanked him. Only later did the important symbolism of his act begin to dawn on me. He had given me the lens that most marked the style of his films (and I would take style as "soul," or a manifestation of it). In effect, he was declaring that he would never work in the cinema again.

Ten years later, I showed him my film, "Dog Star Man," and several others in which I had used that lens. I had whirled that lens and turned it so that the world is revolving, shooting up and whirling. Sidney was very pleased that his lens had been used and said to me in his flat voice, "Well, I used it vertically and horizontally, so all that was left to do was to turn it."

Of all the brilliant people in film that I have met or heard of, none is more intelligent that Sidney Peterson. His intellect and his shyness are his two greatest strengths. The naivete exists in his work, and yet it is extremely ordered in terms of intellect; either would be unbearable unless tempered by the other. One can see that he was a man not too different from Duchamp, and that at some point in his life he developed a balance similar to that artist's.

The time did arrive in his life when his perfection of the medium had reached such a point, that to make one more film would have been unbearable. That is, his intellect would take over and create an imbalance. When that point arrived, he gave up film as an art form or as an independent personal expression and began seeking ways to exercise his faculties, more publicly at first and, finally, in absolute privacy.

Photo: Joel Singer

James Broughton

I would like to give the first word to James Broughton, by quoting excerpts from the forward to his book of collected poems, *A Long Undressing*, published by Jargon. The title is taken from Walter de La Mare's poem:

> They say death's a going to bed; I doubt it;
> but anyhow life's a long undressing.

The foreword is titled "I Am a Medium," and it is written in blank verse. It's a biographical statement which James wrote especially for *A Long Undressing*:

> I am not a Small, a Large, or an XL.
> I am not long or short, raw or well done.
> I am an M, a Medium, a Regular.
> I am a Medium. But I like high mass and low dives,
> sunsets and serpents, old wine and new wrinkles,
> top drawers and getting to the bottom of things. . . .
>
> My grandfathers were bankers, and so was my father.
> But my mother wanted me to become a surgeon.
> However, one night when I was 3 years old
> I was awakened by a glittering stranger

who told me I was a poet and always would be
and never to fear being alone or being laughed at.
That was my first meeting with my angel
who is the most interesting poet I have ever met.

My childhood passions were dancing and swimming,
circuses, amusement parks, movies, vaudeville,
the Book of Knowledge and the land of Oz.
Pet playthings: my toy theater, my magic lantern.
When I was 10 I was sent away to military school.
There my angel came to my rescue:
I fell madly in love with the English language
(And also the captain of the baseball team.)
My favorite book is still Webster's Unabridged, 2nd ed. . . .

I have benefited from generous initiators.
Robert Duncan introduced me to the hermetic circle.
Madeline Gleason introduced me to poetry reading.
Adrian Wilson introduced me to fine printing.
Sidney Peterson introduced me to filmmaking.
Anais Nin introduced me to Anais Nin.
Joseph Henderson introduced me to C.G. Jung.
Alan Watts introduced me to metaphysics. . . .

I have enjoyed collaborations with many artists:
designers, performers, photographers, composers.
But I owe a special long salute to Kermit Sheets,
my sidekick and fellow conspirator for over 20 years.
In 1948 we started the Centaur Press in our basement
where Kermit printed handsome books of poetry.
His first: my verse play, *The Playground*,
which he also produced at the Interplayers theater.
Other Centaur books of mine from Kermit's hand:

> *The Ballad of Mad Jenny* (in violet wrappers)
> and *Musical Chairs* (with Lee Mullican drawings).
>
> In this same period we were making experimental films for Art in Cinema with the help of Frank Stauffacher. Cinema has been for me a gratifying extension of poetry since it can put imaginary toads into real gardens. . . .

When I arrived in San Francisco in the early 1950s, James was rather a legend. I stayed in the basement of his house, the old Centaur Press at 1724 Baker Street. The walls of my room were lined with James's library. Any time you see a house in one of Broughton's movies, it is probably 1724 Baker Street, or some building close by. It is an old frame house that had survived the earthquake at the turn of the century, and it had passed on from artist to artist and, for all I know, is still being passed on thus. The basement room also contained Broughton's films, which he had left behind when he went to Europe.

One fact that he alludes to in his poetic forward is that he was gay. In those days to be homosexual meant risking beatings from anyone who felt like it, including the police. It possibly meant long jail sentences, up to ten years. It meant complete ostracism from family, it meant loss of your job, etc. There was a reign of terror against homosexuality such as is difficult to imagine today. Any man who read books, or spoke in a high-pitched voice, or was loving in his feelings toward the world at large, was suspect. And to be suspected of homosexuality then was to be guilty.

You cannot say that James Broughton escaped this, but he certainly dealt with it in a direct way. In the first place, he knew that to be gay did not necessarily mean to be just one thing. Broughton could make love with women also, and he did. He could be both masculine and feminine in whatever the relationship, and this gave him great strength as an artist. It gave him a much fuller view of the world, and it gave him his central concern, which was to deal with both sides of any matter. So yin-yang came to him as a natural symbol, not one imposed by the mysterious East. The attraction of opposites was always clear to him.

Kermit Sheets was James's lover. They lived together at 1724 Baker Street and turned out a wonderful series of books. Sheets was the first one to publish Robert Duncan's poetry, as well as that of many other poets in the San Francisco circle. Broughton has this to say of that time: "We lived together because we worked together; we printed books; we produced plays; we made films. The press was a source of income. We shared the tasks that had to be done. Kermit is still one of my closest friends and knows me better than I know myself. The important thing is that he was a perfect collaborator for me at that time. Kermit helped me to realize my own vision, and I have paid tribute to him and to this aspect in my Forward to the book [*A Long Undressing*]."

So Broughton was reticent, as his whole generation always will be, with regard to homosexuality. However, that is not too much different from being shy because an angel appeared in a dream when he was three years old and told him he was a poet, something which most people would find difficult to believe. It probably would be taken as an indication of madness, if not just simply as a metaphor. It is not a metaphor. All his life Broughton had visions and visitations. He has always been very open about this, and not in the least pompous. His attitude toward these visions, visitations and appearances was to take them very much for granted; he did not attempt to build a religion around them. But he has always been very frank about describing visitations in a very beautiful fashion. A lovely example is in these few verses from his poem "The Night Watch of the Magdalene," which was published as part of the collection in *A Long Undressing*:

On the long outskirts of a dismantled city
toward the final flicker of dusk

I entered the nave of an unfinished cathedral
and sought Mary Magdalene cooking up a stew,
the stove a glow as red as her hair
and a three-forked spoon in her hand.

Dear lady, my feet ache, I said to her,
I've come all the way from my Dad's hometown
    trying to find his footsteps.

Have a sip of chowder, sir, said she,
I've been stirring and poking this pot for years,
it won't cure at all, nor is it lethal,
it's rich in folly and savors of rue
but it sometimes helps in the middle of the night.

A man risks his reputation by publishing *A Long Undressing*. It was published in 1972 by Jonathan Williams at considerable risk. Why? Because Broughton's poetry is not "in" by any stretch of the imagination:

Papa has a pig.
And a big pig too.
Papa plays a piggy-toe that I can't do.
O Papa has the biggest pig you ever did see.
He gave only ten little piggies to me.
    Papa has the star of all the swine,
    Papa shines stern in the sty.

Now, we all know enough about American poetry in the 20th century to know that these have been probably the most unpopular, spat-upon, dismissed, ignored poems ever written. Broughton just never "fit in" with any movement — not even those he hatched himself.

However, he got along well with people, and they would be delighted with his poetry in spite of themselves but still would say, "What *is* all this damned nonsense?" We were all under the shadow of T.S. Eliot's *The Wasteland* then, and if not that, certainly under the huger and more authentic shadow of Ezra Pound's *Cantos*; or under the influence of the kind of humor and intellectualization that characterized Gertrude Stein. Whereas Broughton always insisted on being fey, or gay, or flippant. He would flip the language this way and that, and put it into meters that were considered "done with" a century ago; yet it would somehow work.

Despite themselves, the people "on the scene" would continue to come back to Broughton's poems, but no one dared risk his reputation by attempting to get them into print as Jonathan Williams did. Far-out, avant-garde, "searching-for-new-ways" people often have the most conservative attitudes toward anything that will not fit in with their movement. Really, my experience with artists has been that, generally speaking, one-half step outside their own field and they are much more conservative and malicious than George Bush. As a result of this attitude, Broughton was largely ignored — as much as one could ignore someone as lively as he.

James and Kermit also staged plays; Kermit became quite a well known director in San Francisco theaters. Broughton wrote plays that were always liked by the public and, perhaps for that reason, were damned by the circle of poets: damned with faint praise.

Films were another matter. Film had no art circle at that time. There was no little art crowd touting what was the latest against the other little art crowd touting the opposite latest. Film was still outside this kind of clutch. Broughton found great release in making films, much as Cocteau did. I think Cocteau was a great inspiration to him. Broughton thought of his own films as cine-poems. He read his poems on the soundtracks of many of them, although the images were not illustrations of the poems; but you might say, they do a dance with them. There was great freedom for him in this aspect of filmmaking.

Kermit Sheets is the man at the beginning of Broughton's film "Mother's Day," who is holding a box of candy in one hand and a mandolin in the other and shaking them. Kermit became a central figure in Broughton's films, as was the case of Jean Daste and Jean Vigo. Kermit was quite the opposite of James, but he could act out aspects of Broughton's vision, like the Pan nature of "Loony Tom."

I want to say something about Broughton's childhood — rather, we will let him speak for himself on that subject:

> "It would really be accurate to say that I was persecuted by my parents for three things: for my innate delicacy of manner and feeling, for masturbating, and (most wounding of all) for my first intense experience of love — since the object of this love was that very 'captain of the baseball team,' that strong blond older boy who taught me what reciprocal love could be. This happened away from home, when I was in the military school. My parents sent me away to school when I was ten years old because they did not want me to be a sissy. As my mother said to me, 'You are too sensitive for this world.' She often said this through the years. It made me wonder what world I belonged in, and where it was. In any event, when she discovered my love affair, which had been going on for two years, she withdrew me from the school in midterm, brought me home, and kept me locked in. I was 15 years old then. . . ."

Broughton was locked in a tower, one of those types of architecture you see again and again in his films. These square towers are common in the San Francisco Bay area; there was one in the home of his parents, where he was imprisoned. It was an incredibly mythic thing to do to him. There are only a few consequences when parents have taken that extreme stance. One leads to becoming a "closet queen" for the rest of your life and concealing your sexuality; the other leads to becoming what Broughton became. His repression in childhood served toward the development of an extraordinary imagination. He grew up and wrote poetry, and made films in which sexuality was a primary subject.

He says, "Sexuality in its varied forms, its play, its vitality, its proliferations, etc., as manifestations of the life impulse – that has always been inherent in my vision, and is true to my Scorpio nature."

Because of the constant repression and persecution of his sexuality, Broughton came to make a prominent place for sexuality in his art; and this then became a defense of sexuality, which is the main thrust of his work. Actually, his films were very much more shocking when they were first shown than they are now. It is difficult for young people to conceive of the extent of repression of sexuality at that time. Maybe the best "fix" on this is the silliness of Hollywood movies of the day. Broughton preys on this. For example, in the beginning of his film "Mother's Day" he is paying homage to Chaplin's "City Lights," which begins with Chaplin in the lap of the statue.

Throughout Broughton's work you will find very intentional and specific allusions to early comedies. I think that the mother in "Mother's Day" in her younger version, particularly when she keeps entering the room and taking off her shawl, is the spitting image of Georgia Hale who played the girl in "The Gold Rush."

At the time Broughton made the film, "Mother's Day," art in San Francisco was a very private and personal affair, as it always finally is; but there was no public art crowd *per se*, at least none publicly interested in San Francisco artists. The artists formed a private family-of-interest among themselves and, while there were "family squabbles," the artists were mostly very friendly to each other. This atmosphere helped James to create those qualities peculiar to his films, of natural home-moviemaking. He was the first man to "father" those qualities into an aesthetic filmic formalism – a traditional, even theatrical formalism.

Once San Francisco was discovered as an "art scene," this family of artists scattered and many friendships disintegrated. People who had been very close friends started picketing each other's readings and exhibits and film shows. I lived to see the day when one of

Robert Duncan's closest friends, Jack Spicer, put a picket sign at one of Duncan's readings, saying, "Robert Duncan has sold out. Robert Duncan is chi-chi."

One of the problems with the arts in America is that when they emerge into public prominence, they are regarded as a kind of football or basketball game. You must have two teams, and one must win over the other. Then you must play again next year and hope that the team that lost this year will win, because everybody is for the underdog. Always there is the idea of teams – "Abstract" vs. "Realistic," etc. But in that great beautiful melting pot that San Francisco was in those days, there were Abstract Realists and Realistic Abstractionists, and on and on. What would one call "Mother's Day," for example? A drama? A poem? A musical?

The friendliness, the family-of-artists, all came to an end when poetry came into the public arena and people were forced to defend their particular aesthetic against another. It was squabble, squabble, squabble, from then on.

Yet there is certainly enough poetry to go around, for every sensibility; and Broughton's poetry could have been accepted if it had been given a chance. But after a century of being beaten over the head with Walt Whitman and other free verse writers, it is almost impossible for rhymed verse to be "in."

The photo of Broughton on the jacket of *A Long Undressing* is a good one. It was taken by Imogen Cunningham. She expressed him with a double head, one looking at the other. This is very effective, because Broughton's face divides more amazingly than any person I know. One side is quite young and innocent and boyish looking. The other side is almost demonic; the lines are etched much deeper, the face is not nearly as smooth, and the mouth is almost fanged by the creases at the end. This split is expressive of his personality: Blake's *The Marriage of Heaven and Hell* is one of his favorite books.

Broughton attempts to make a bridge between the black humor of surrealism and Freudian humor, all the way to the early comedies of Chaplin, Keaton and Sennett. He did not want one or the other, he wanted to be a bridge in the sense of "Heaven and Hell," and I think he is the only man who succeeded. He is the only artist of late in film whom I find rooted specifically in the early Golden Age of comedy, as it is called. But he has achieved a much greater depth of intelligence in his art.

The Freudian analogies, the symbolic analogies, of "Mother's Day" are fairly simple, but they are used masterfully, and you cannot help but admire his handling of allusion after allusion with such wit and grace – no heavy-handedness. The circle in the egg, the foot in the boot, the hat business. You see, Broughton would take his cues from, say, "Steamboat Bill, Jr.," where Buster Keaton as a young man is taken into the store by his father to choose a hat: one hat is too big, one too small, one goes on this way, one goes on that way, and finally it is hilarious. We laugh very simply; we laugh without thinking too much about why we are laughing.

Broughton has thought about why people laugh, and he has put the hat into "Mother's Day" at the level of understanding what is funny about it. It is very simple. Whenever you have repression, the thing being repressed will break out in any way it can find. If a little boy is not supposed to think of his penis, then he will look past his penis down to his toes. His toes will very soon become a substitute for his penis, and he will play with his toes. The next step is that, being blocked from finding out what his penis can and is supposed to do, he will find out by, for instance, putting his foot into the shoe. This hatches all sorts of weird variations. It is amazing that people blocked at finding something will find some other way to it. Health will out! Mother Nature has her way!

Broughton's first few films were each quite different; the first, "The Potted Psalm," with Sidney Peterson, then "Mother's Day" and "The Adventures of Jimmy." Each of these was distinctly different from the others, steps in Broughton's development.

Then came a series of related films, "Loony Tom," "Four in the Afternoon," culminating in "The Pleasure Garden." I think that in this last series Broughton was a little trapped as an artist. He had great variation, but he wasn't growing much.

Let me say, however, that one has to honor this kind of aesthetic "trap." Domenico Scarlatti, for instance, became utterly "trapped" in the sonata form, and used a tiny harpsichord with a very limited keyboard. He went to the Spanish Court and spent the rest of his life writing harpsichord sonatas. But Scarlatti was a supreme artist because he took very simple qualities of sound and rhythm and varied them for the rest of his life; and you want to hear everything he wrote and hear each piece many times. The same is true of Broughton's films of this early-to-mid period. If you really love these films, you will start to admire the variations he's managed within this "tight" form. When you look at this series of films — "Loony Tom" through "The Pleasure Garden" — again and again, you will find it is an art of the variation that Broughton was involved with, rather than a growth in the art.

One can see how out of the contemporary scene this put Broughton. He is in an age when an artist is expected to grow and grow in his art and then suddenly arrive at a certain level of public acceptance and stay there the rest of his life, so that a gallery owner or impresario can sell his work easily. Broughton is a man who quickly stated his platform, performed his variations, and *then* grew.

When I arrived in San Francisco, I asked, "Where is Broughton?" He was such a great figure in the art circles that his absence was obvious. I learned that he and Kermit Sheets had gone to Europe. Broughton's films were receiving recognition abroad, and he thought Europe would be a congenial atmosphere in which to live and to learn more of the history of cinema.

They remained in Europe for four years. As James says, "I was very happy in Europe and very tempted to settle permanently in England, where I was treated with great respect and offered many opportunities to work. But the climate eventually undid me."

In England (and with the same drive that propelled Peterson in New York), Broughton tried to break out of the closed circle of private art into a publicly recognized art. He did very well in London at this time; got backing and started making "The Pleasure Garden," to be released commercially in all the art houses. The film was made outdoors, with professional actors in many of the leading parts. It was hoped that "The Pleasure Garden" would become popular like, say, post-war British comedies — that it would be shown all around the world and make money, and Broughton would be famous. Then the money ran out and he sank most of the rest of his own fortune into finishing the film. It was completed and sent back to America; and he returned at that time also.

"The Pleasure Garden" won a prize at Cannes and various other film festivals here and in Europe. Then it opened in New York in a little theater — and failed. It was just too good for that time. Maybe, if it were released now it would succeed; but even now it is too strange, too weird a work to become popular. It is filled with anxious wit — it is ratchety. The viewer finds himself laughing, but at the same time is disturbed. So it was not a success commercially, and this was a great disappointment to Broughton.

He had enough money left to settle back into San Francisco, but he had decided that he would make no more films. He had a bitterness for many years which, I think, was as extreme as Sidney Peterson's. He was "through" with filmmaking. He went on writing poetry and plays, but if you mentioned films, his brow would wrinkle and furrow. He was totally discouraged because he felt that films for him were doomed to remain a strictly personal matter. It took him about ten years to get over this. All of us pleaded with him to make another film, and I was certainly among the loudest.

During this time, I had moved away from San Francisco, and was living in Colorado. In 1961, I asked James to come out to Colorado for a three-day festival in his honor. Nothing like that had been done before, and he was delighted. Jane and I had gone to five different student groups to raise the support and receive assurances that they would present all of his films, that his plays would be presented by student players, and that the poetry groups would present him as a poet. We raised a good deal of money and put on his plays. Jane memorized all of "Mad Jenny" and performed it as a monologue. Broughton had a great time, and the students loved him — in fact, he is just naturally lovable at his public appearances. We had a great session. He stayed in our house. We had three children — one baby and two just getting around — in a mountain cabin, and he was very taken with our way of life.

Then he invited me to San Francisco. He had arranged that I should give some lectures at some of the local colleges. I stayed at his place, and it seemed to me that he kept trying to seduce me. Finally, I made it clear to him that homosexuality, in terms of going to bed with him, did not interest me. So there was a great deal of just plain honest talk between us, and observations of the mechanics of love, in an attempt to straighten out what had otherwise become an impossible tangle of contradiction in our relationship.

Broughton was heavily into Jungian analysis then, and had been for some time. His analyst was the man to whom C.G. Jung had handed "the keys" to take to America. So Broughton had undergone a great deal of analysis, and it had done a great deal for him. Much of this informs his later poems. He was very consciously and intellectually out to resolve opposites. He lived his life with a certain kind of perfection.

But he was still discouraged about making films until, finally, Jacques Ledoux handed him a thousand feet of color film, and that gesture was sufficient for him to make "The Bed."

He had, however, made another film, after about five or six years of his discouragement, "Nuptiae," which was not released until after "The Bed" was made and released. Broughton says of "Nuptiae": "This was not made to be a film. It was conceived of as a 'home movie' record. Only much later did I consider shaping it into art."

"The Bed" naturally follows "Nuptiae," because it has everything that "Nuptiae" does *not* — about loving, whereas "Nuptiae" is concerned only about the rituals and ceremonies of marriage. "The Bed" made Broughton famous overnight and was shown in theaters all over the country. Everyone in "The Bed" is naked and beautifully so, and it is uproariously funny and easily so, and it accomplished everything for James that he had thought "The Pleasure Garden" would.

James says that it was only after the success of "The Bed" and his renewed interest in film, that he considered doing anything with the "Nuptiae" footage. He used almost all the footage, and it took him a year to edit and release it. James is the star of the film, and his own loving pretentiousness and sincerity in the filmed ceremony and attending rituals is its great strength, its trump card.

It happens that I helped James to make "Nuptiae" — I did the photography. I had returned to Colorado from the lecture tour in San Francisco and I was very excited about the city. I wanted to live there again. So I took the whole family, driving cross-country in an old car with a U-Haul trailer, with seven cats and all the dice rolled against us. We arrived in town and ended up in a cockroach-ridden, utterly horrible place in the Mission District. I started to look for work and began getting asthma attacks, and got sicker and sicker. I had no job and no way to support my family.

In the meantime, James had been courting a woman for some time. She was an artist and designer, originally from Kansas, who was then working for the San Francisco Opera. Her name was Suzanna — Suzy. One day James came over to our miserable flat and said, "I'm going to marry Suzanna and I want it to be the most poetic wedding ceremony that has ever occurred in America. I am going to spend the rest of my money on it." He mentioned Sir Francis Bacon who had done this, and he intended to emulate him, and by that gesture rid himself of his whole past; or, as he said, "transform the past and hopefully enter into a new dimension of human experience."

They had a civil ceremony in the gorgeous San Francisco City Hall. Then he invited his closest friends to meet "up the Coast" at a house designed by Frank Lloyd Wright which was being run by two old friends as a resort. Some of us went early to work for several days on the ceremony. Alan Watts came to collaborate with James on the words of the ceremony. Jane and I went along because James had said that it was the relationship of Jane and me which had inspired him to fulfill the "other half" of his life, and his Jungian analyst who had made it possible for him to do so.

The film "Nuptiae" has a serious tone and is in a serious setting, and yet this is what contributes so much to its black-comedy aspects. The humor within the solemnity of the marriage ceremony is central to this film's concerns. You don't really have to know the background of the film if you just have a chance to look at it about five times. Take yourself back to Laurel and Hardy, or "The Andalusian Dog," and then look at "Nuptiae" in that context.

The music of the film becomes funny, within its seriousness. Lou Harrison's music has this beautiful sense of pontificating; but it also clashes and clangs in a way that is uproarious if you are listening for the hysterical humor of it.

I appeared in the film as "shaggy man" at the wedding and photographed the civil ceremony, and then we all met at the place way up on the Mendocino coast. The day we arrived the fog settled down over everything and stayed there. The sun never shone, so one element that Broughton had been counting on, by the gods removed — the sun. (You see, we plan all these works of art, as well as ceremonies, selfishly; and the gods assist with counter-balances.) Then Alan Watts arrived, the self-defrocked priest. When he applied to the local Catholic church for permission to borrow certain instruments to be used in the ceremony, such as a Communion cup, they refused; but, fortunately, James had brought one with him.

So there we were in a house that is supposed to be sunny, filled with happiness and light, with people preparing for a wedding, and there was no sun but rather a fog all around and a good deal of nervousness. We are sunk in the forest with the sea booming down below, in a house full of religious objects.

Alan and James were busy polishing the details of the wedding ceremony. It was to have all the elements of ceremonies from all around the world and from all different cultures. But it has been a great delusion in America that you can take a little bit of this religion and a dash of that, and a sprinkling of many religious cultures, and pull them all together into one religion. Instead, you have a big (sometimes black) mass, because many of these religions are naturally antagonistic and directly opposed to each other. In "Nuptiae" you see a Buddha in his stance, accompanied by a church bell, followed by the Virgin Mary, the harp, etc. – it is like a United Nations of marriage ceremonies. Broughton intended it to be a universal statement enacted poetically; he believes in living poetically, not just writing poetry.

In the ceremony, Suzanna's Jungian psychiatrist gives her away (that is the woman with the white hair piled on her head), and James's Jungian psychiatrist gives him away (that is the fearful old man with the glasses who often looks dour). The best man is Kermit Sheets; he is older than in the earlier films, has glasses, and his hair is graying; but it is still Loony Tom at heart. Alan Watts's son-in-law is playing the harp ("with a bow on the arp," as Pound would characterize it). There are candles burning all over the place, which were a constant hazard because the building was made of wood. Everyone was rather apprehensive, and yet they are all smiling and taking proper wedding stances and being properly concerned. These tensions come out clearly watching Alan Watts as "the priest." He is a riot. He is performing the ceremony with an absolutely straight face, and there are extremely subtle moments when his face goes completely blank.

I am photographing, of course, and actually appear for a brief instant. Two of my children are flower carriers. We even had a satyr type in attendance, the same old man who sits on the tree and blows his trumpet in "The Bed." He had, for this ceremony, curled his white hair so that it made little horns, and he was dancing around, playing the bongo drums. Try to put a harp with bongo drums. So this is the atmosphere in which "Nuptiae" was filmed. Broughton was completely sincere all the way through, and it took him a year to discover that it was another, newer, Broughton film. At that point he could edit it and release it.

Watching "Nuptiae," one is struck by the little gestures — they are of such subtlety! James intends to take Suzanna's hand as a Renaissance gentleman would, and instead fumbles and the fingers move toward a loving stroke. His love of her overcomes all formality, and makes his hand break down in the gesture — just as the film breaks up into much more than he had intended.

James planned that we should all go down to the beach so that he and Suzanna could enact certain symbolic rituals with "the Great Mother, the Sea" — a sacrifice with a golden ball and some flags, during which he and Suzy were to take off their clothes. So it had not been quite decided when we went down to photograph this whether she would strip or whether he would, or what. (Broughton termed this "casting off, symbolically, of an old skin, or outworn garments.") So the time came when he was taking off his clothes and she was making a gesture — and we see a pure Kansas matron in about one half a second. She was just not able to perform the "symbolic" action. James "followed suit," stripping only to his bathing trunks.

Next, James is casting away a box of old love letters from his past. The box also contained some objects that were difficult for him to part with. He had carried them around for years. He threw the box into the sea; and it floated and then started coming back and lodged between two rocks. He said, "Cut," and I stopped the camera. He picked up the box — because he was determined to complete the drama — and threw it farther out and said, "Go ahead"; so I started shooting again. (I was very much subservient to the kind of film I thought he wanted.) The box repeated its pattern, though, and this time I went on photographing it. The message of the gods was clear – that you do not, just by burning things or throwing things away, get rid of the past. If a man really wanted a box to be carried out to sea, his subconscious would find the current that would carry it there. Broughton found the current that would bring it back. This is intrinsic to his whole cyclical sense of life. He was to sustain his marriage, but he could not really change his life. No one can. However, to quote James, "He can attempt to enlarge it, enrich it, and endure it!"

"Nuptiae" is a very tragi-comic film. The minute you can begin to laugh at it, the next evolution is to realize what an incredibly sad film it also is. It is sad because of the great sincerity with which it was conceived and made, as contrasted with the effect upon the viewer who is not aware that it is indeed a serious ceremony or does not have the benefit of the knowledge of the poetic symbolism that went into planning it. The final result is a parody. It is well-known that serious home movies become the cause of hilarious laughter at a later date – because human pretension is always funny as well as sad. When you watch "Nuptiae," keep your eyes open, because it is a hell of a comedy.

Still, as far as Broughton was concerned, this marriage was a very serious business. He would say, "This is the most serious thing I have done in my entire life." The costumes were very elaborate and of costly material. Suzanna, a professional designer, designed them, so they were gorgeous. The flags were made with great thought to the minutest detail of symbolism, in balance and proportion, and they were meticulously sewn. Jane had been sewing while I was photographing. A great deal of thought was given to all the objects that were used. All the statues were actually museum pieces. I did not shoot them as such; I shot a great deal more than are in the finished film, but I think they became overwhelming to the continuities of the film itself. James must have begun to be uncertain about things that he saw were incongruous in terms of the seriousness of the ceremony – which was his first consideration. So in the final edited film, he added yin-yang symbols, ancient Indian drawings, etc., in superimposition. He wanted to make a transpersonal statement about the union of opposites – to take the film beyond the merely private record.

If "Nuptiae" cannot be viewed now by audiences detached from personal considerations as one of the great "black-comedy" parodies of film, it has no merit except as an historical record for those concerned in its making. Because no matter what the sincerity, solemnity, symbolism, poetic fervor or emotional need with which it was made, it still comes through as a comedy, or perhaps as a tragi-comedy, and this is what makes it great. And Broughton, in editing it, has again shown his great courage and the soul of an artist.

The beautiful thing about this film is that Broughton permits himself, at the most serious moment in is life – when he is staking the ultimate in terms of money, in terms of sex, in terms of his career – to go overboard and become intensely ostentatious, even pompous; and he finally has the courage to admit this and edit the film. He had to grow through marriage to reach this point, so that the artist could take over.

Of course "Nuptiae" stands on its own without explanation. In fact, it should be said that James disagrees totally with my interpretation of this film. But I would like to say a few more things about its filming and his editing of it. I can see, for example, the order of things his subconscious presented to the artist working. For instance, the flags were shot before the ceremony; that is, between the two ceremonies; and he cut to that shot of mine of the ghostly black rocks in the sea of white, all curling and tilting and ominous. He cut to that shot right from the wedding banquet. Everyone is laughing and crying, eating and drinking and loving, and then he cut to life at its bleakest. The only thing more blunt that he could have done would be to inset a title reading, "The Morning After."

Then come these two courageous little figures with the flags they have made themselves. In James's poetic vision this symbolized "going to the sea to make offerings to the Great Deep, for renewal and rebirth." This is foolishness, but you have to expand the meaning of the word "foolish" to include wonderful human courage. If you represent the whole universe as a huge auditorium and the world as a tiny bee-bee in that auditorium, and on that bee-bee put these minute creatures – then you have the proportions and perspective of this film at this instant. That is comedy at its wittiest – "at wit's end" – and blackest . . . and whitest.

Remember that James had waited for the sun to come out – and it didn't. There was no time left, so we had to photograph on this bleak, fog-bound day; and still here they come with their flags.

I chose the speeds at which the shots were taken; so I have James and Suzy coming down the hill in slow motion. Then they start playing ball, which I speeded up so that comedy enters just by the hilarity of the movement – humans reduced to some tiny creature-ness in speeded motion (as they are, say, "given weight" during slow-motion sequences). Then comes a great moment: they are throwing the ball back and forth, and James drops it and it rolls down to the sea. He runs to get it and does something which, for me, is the high point in the film. Instead of just reaching down or splashing into the water to get the ball, he stands with arms outstretched, and the ball is brought to him by the waves. There is an edge flare on the film which occurs because the roll of film was running out at that moment; but Broughton had the sensibility to leave that flare in, with the effect that he gestures with raised arms and the ball is brought back to him in an orange flame. This is – and I will say it surely! – a high point in cinema in terms of human feeling and understanding of the human condition.

There are three levels to the ceremony in the film. One is obedience to the state – the laws of the land – as exemplified by the courthouse. Second is obedience to the laws of history and tradition, which you share most properly with your friends. The third is a matter between husband and wife. It is interesting that whereas most people would relate the third to bed, James did not. He related it in a much larger metaphor — that of renunciation, which he takes as ritual also.

James Broughton has lived a much fuller life since his marriage. He has two children, a son and a daughter. His film "This Is It" is a portrait of his son and shows his love for the child.

Again, a poem from *A Long Undressing*, the poem which James liked especially to read to Suzanna:

"The Girl with the Beady Black Eyes"

She was my honey baby, she sure was my delight
  with her beautiful beady black eyes.
I met her in Modesto in the middle of the night
  when the old hotel burned down.

Her name was Ida Lee, she stood blushing in a fright
  with her beautiful beady black eyes.
She had come from San Francisco just to pass the night
  But the old hotel burned down.

In her lace and pinky nightgown she looked a rosy sight
  with her beautiful beady black eyes.
I saved her from the flames in the middle of the night
  when the old hotel burned down.

She is still my honey babe, though her hair is turning white
  with her beautiful beady black eyes.
In our San Francisco home we often laugh about the night
  when the old hotel burned down,
    when the whole town burned to hell.

"The Bed" is what we call a "magic work"; that is, one of those works which — after you bust your ass-thetics getting everything right, learning all the techniques, worrying about every detail — comes like a gift from the gods: you are finally permitted to make a magic work. This falls out for every filmmaker now and again. A "magic work" is a film that "works" on all levels. It can be very popular, as "The Bed" was, and it can be seen again and again. You can have a copy of "The Bed" in your home, as I do, and look at it many times, and it still informs. It is still exciting. These "magic works" are very rare, and can properly be called "masterpieces."

"The Bed" shows the ritual of "bed" in all its manifestations — all the basic uses of the bed, except dreamless sleeping. So this film was the logical film for James to make before editing "Nuptiae"; and I think he made it quite freely.

For this film he had another cameraman, a good one, a student of his, I believe. He had begun teaching in order to make a living for his family, and Suzanna had opened a craft shop which she operated. By this time they had had their children, daughter Serena and son Orion.

With "The Bed," Broughton made a genuine return to film-making. He followed it with "The Golden Positions," which pays homage to the tradition of nakedness, as a natural follow-up or corollary to "The Bed." Then comes "This Is It," his filmic homage to the creation of children, now very much a part of his life.

Looking at these films diligently, you can draw a full sense of Broughton's life (and perhaps one opposite to my own perception). All I ever ask of any work is that it is true to itself, and that is all I ever ask of a person, too. I can get along with just about anyone who is himself or herself.

For instance, I totally disagree with Broughton's life style — it doesn't really interest me. But that is also why I love him — because he is opposite from me. His films, of course, are totally opposite from mine — about as opposite as you can get. There are filmmakers whose lives are a matter of indifference to me; and yet when I look at their film works I can understand something of their lives and can sympathize with them. That is the beauty of Art; whether you know the artist personally or not, if you become involved with his work, you know him.

Critics have a lot of trouble knowing artists for that very reason. They always want to locate the whole thing in a perfect work of art – which is, anyway, beyond human consideration. Then when they meet the shabby, shuffling, dumb, stupid, "spit-running-from-his-mouth," ignorant, begging, insistent artist, they get very upset. It is because they cannot see either the artist or his work in human terms. (I am, by the way, describing myself with that picture of the artist – that's very much the way I appear when I'm working.) Most critics tend to keep backing up into their shells – many teachers, also – getting more and more introspective until they can no longer realize there are an infinite number of arts, as there are people. The only thing that makes a work qualify as an art is if it is true to itself and reveals as much as it pretends to.

Yes, of course, there are many very articulate critics interested in film. Annette Michelson, for instance, a brilliant woman, one of the great critics in the country and of a very human quality. And Jonas Mekas. It only takes a *living* relationship with a work of art – or an artist – to make any work live up to its "greatest expectations." This is the case with James Broughton's work; look at his films – look at "The Bed," at "Nuptiae," then "The Bed" once more, and look at how he made these works and how he lies in them to get at the Truth.

Photo: Joseph Rostin

Maya Deren

How can a little girl born in Russia and reared in Syracuse, New York, find happiness as a Voodoun priestess in Greenwich Village? That question sort of sums up the story of Maya Deren, who was one of the most complex and legendary personalities among independent filmmakers of the 1940s and 50s.

The facts of Maya Deren's early life are well documented in the first volume of *The Legend of Maya Deren*, published by Anthology Film Archives: She was born Eleanora Derenkowski in Russia, in 1917. Her family fled to this country in 1922 as a result of the Revolution. Her father, Solomon, was a noted psychiatrist and thinker. Maya attended Syracuse University, where she became involved in politics and joined the Trotskyist Young People's Socialist League. She also met the political activist Gregory Bardacke there, and married him when she was eighteen. They moved to New York, where she finished her B.A. at New York University. It was while she was at NYU that she became interested in photography and film. By 1938, Maya and Gregory were divorced, and a year later she received her M.A. in English from Smith College.

One of the early legends of Maya Deren has it that, during her involvement with the Young People's Socialist League, she was sent to Oregon to be the secretary for some lumberjacks who were trying to organize a strike. They failed under pressure from the bosses, and she was the only one left and threw herself into the effort and single-handedly organized a wildcat strike that was successful. There has been a lot of debate whether this is a true story, but anyone who ever met Maya, as I had, or simply seen her films – and you can still feel her intense energy coming through her work – would believe that she was able to do such a thing.

For a number of years, until the late 1930s, she was a socialist and very involved in socialist politics – which, in the eyes of her father, who had fled the Russian Revolution, must have been the most appalling thing she could have been involved in. Nevertheless, she always idolized her father; she kept a picture of him on the wall of her editing room, and as she once told me, she always had a desire to please him. Now, most young women do want to please their fathers, but Maya also had an overwhelming desire to create something that would meet with his approval and respect. He was a very severe, patriarchal man. As I remember, she described him as looking like the Smith Brothers on the cough-drop box – bearded and stern and nineteenth-century. And very hard to please.

Maya never did quite make peace with her father while he was alive. And certainly there were many occasions when her mother would come to shows and the two would end up screaming at each other in Russian out in the lobby.

There was another man who was driven from his land – Alexander Hackenschmied, who fled his native Czechoslovakia in the 1930s as a result of Hitler's advance. Sasha Hammid – as he became known – already had a reputation as a brilliant young motion picture photographer. In America, he was hired by "The March of Time," one of the most important producers of motion-picture news shorts which played in all the local movie theaters. He and Maya met in Los Angeles, where she had moved with her mother. (Her parents had separated and divorced shortly after her marriage to Bardacke.) At the time, Maya was working as the secretary and assistant to Katherine Dunham, the choreographer. In 1942, she and Sasha were married.

Ultimately, she wasn't really happy as a married woman. Certainly, she had no ambition toward being a housewife. She was, at the time, struggling to continue her writing – she had written and published poetry, stories, newspaper articles and essays, including an essay on religious possession in dancing, a subject which would later become a crucial aspect of her life.

But with Sasha, her life as a filmmaker really began. Early in their marriage, she and Sasha decided to make a personal film; so in 1943, "Meshes of the Afternoon" was created. It was a one-of-a-kind film, and still is.

Essentially, Hammid was the photographer; but the real force of the film came from Maya herself. In fact, it's always been assumed that "Meshes" was mainly her film; but from knowing her personally and from studying the film, I have good reason to know that it is Sasha's. "Meshes of the Afternoon" shows its European roots. For all the unusual things that happen within the film, its whole style of photography betrays the very slick, polished, penultimate craftsmanship of the old European sensibility for which Sasha was known.

Like many films made in this period, "Meshes" was made out of the necessity of dealing with devastating psychological and personal problems through film. This film was one of the first examples of that kind of treatment, and its influence was such that a unique film art evolved. The only precedence for this quality of art in film would be the so-called avant-garde, or the small personal films, made mostly in France during the teens and 1920s.

Perhaps the most startling thing about this film is the naturalness and ease with which it presents certain psychological symbology. And that, of course, has to do with the fact that Maya almost cut her teeth on such symbols. Her father's life was so involved with them, and she was so involved with her father, that by the time she came to make this film, these things which by other people might be regarded as symbols had become second nature to her. All of Maya's symbolism was very simple. Maya had the capacity to speak more directly about what everyone else was being very pompous about – that is, symbolism, particularly psychological symbolism – than anyone else I ever met. If one underestimates such a talent, then I suggest trying to make a film that uses the obvious psychological symbols like keys and knives as "Meshes" does, and not bring down the house with laughter.

The title, too, is symbolic. "Meshes," I think, expresses in a poetic way the trap; and "afternoon," of course, implies that period just before evening. Perhaps, too, "meshes" is a simple pun on "mess"; certainly Maya's and Sasha's lives together must have devolved to this point by then.

"Meshes" gave Maya the filmmaker's ball, so to speak, and she immediately picked it up and ran with it. She and Sasha moved to New York, where Maya began staging shows where there had been no place to show independently made films, with that same energy wherewith she could have organized a wildcat strike as a teenager. She managed with her stage presence and with her intense organizing abilities to get a film onto a screen so that she could get onto a stage to speak on independent filmmaking; and practically overnight she woke up huge audiences – and, in fact, the national attention – to the possibilities of independently made film.

She took the ball to the Provincetown Playhouse on MacDougall Street, where she had an electrifying show of several films on the playhouse's "dark nights." After the first showing, the place was packed and hundreds had to be turned away. The theater sold out night after night, and it became quite the thing to do in town for six months, to go see "Meshes of the Afternoon" and listen to this crazy woman spouting film art. So that Maya Deren became recognized as someone incredible and extraordinary in film. From these public presentations sprang all kinds of possibilities for film. In fact, I've heard Amos Vogel say that he doesn't know if he could ever have started Cinema 16 in New York had it not been for Maya Deren attracting such enormous attention to independently made private film.

Sasha, meanwhile, was beginning to feel discouraged. Their marriage started to tear apart, and his career may have been on the wane at the time; he was slipping a bit as the breadwinner. And he was not getting the attention for "Meshes" or as a filmmaker that Maya was. So there was a quarrel between them in which he said that she got all the credit for "Meshes," and where did that leave him?

So, as Maya told it to me, she said that they would make another and it would be his.

That film was "The Private Life of a Cat," released in 1946. It is a powerful, explosive film, with as much tension — as much having to do with their struggling marriage — as "Meshes," perhaps more.

Now, Maya and Sasha had no children. They did have cats; and their cats were their children. Everything that had to do with holding the household together was invested in those cats. So that was what they made the film about; the cats were the metaphor, the totem that they most happily shared in the midst of their dissolving marriage.

The film was, of course, a collaboration; and we do see two distinct camera styles in it. Those who have seen "Meshes of the Afternoon" are easily able to spot Sasha's pictures. They are immaculate — as immaculate as can be when the photographer is trying to catch an action down on the floor around the catbox. They bring all of his old-world, sophisticated craftsmanship to a beautiful pitch. Then there are an extraordinary number of shots in which the camera is rachety, where it moves with a particularity of style that is as easily distinct from Sasha's as a brushstroke of Van Gogh is from one of Rembrandt. It is my opinion that these are Maya's shots. There must have been times when Sasha, whose shots took time to set up, was away, times when things were happening that needed to be recorded; so Maya would have had to take the camera. At some point then, they decided which of whose shots should go in, in which order, to make the completed film, the final statement. And the result is that "The Private Life of a Cat" is, in essence, Maya

Deren's first film – at least I am convinced of this after years of studying it. But, of course, it's called Sasha's. Which is one of the ironies of life, that "Meshes," which was his and considered hers, led to "The Private Life" which was hers and considered his.

Unhappily, "The Private Life of a Cat" is shown very seldom. Even retrospectives of Deren's work rarely include it. I think it is one of the finest films that has ever been made, for a number of reasons. One is as the final result of Maya's and Sasha's collaboration. The majority of images are by Sasha; but many of hers shaped his. There are those who disagree with me on the extent of Maya's involvement in shooting this film, but in my opinion only Maya can be responsible, for instance, for those angularities of shot which go up to indicate the cupboard where the mother cat is looking for a place to have its kittens. It's only Sasha who could have made the image where the camera starts with the cat's eye and lifts . . . lifts as with the wings of Phoebus (or the very best of Hollywood dolly shots) up over a box and ends in a superbly crafted composition. One of the most wondrous parts in the film for me is the sequence when the mother cat moves her kittens to a new place. Very possibly, when this happened Maya was the only one home, and picked up the camera and shot it; it's certainly her style of image, to follow the cat in motion, then to make a shift of the whole body into another direction, to make a composition that will accommodate where the cat has led the eye. And Sasha's innercut in the sequence is perfect – his shot of the father cat sitting composed as any old European monarch among his pillows overseeing things. Each of them – both of them – were so concerned with making a good film, that there's no singular egoistic style. And yet the final result, with the editing-in of the different styles of photography, of vision, says so much about him and her.

Now, Maya always had the problem of trying to live up to the expectations of "Meshes," which was so famous. She had this very famous film (for which she was wrongly credited as the main maker

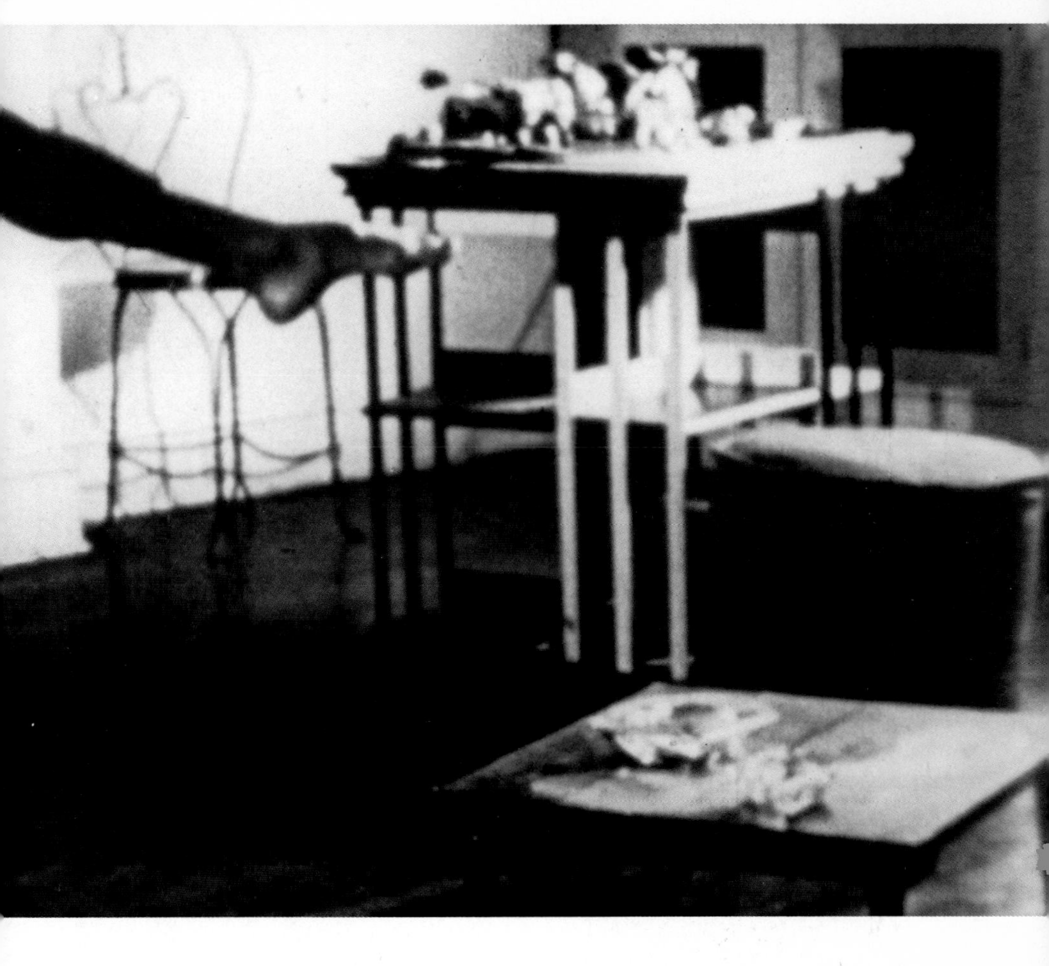

Choreography for Camera by Maya Deren

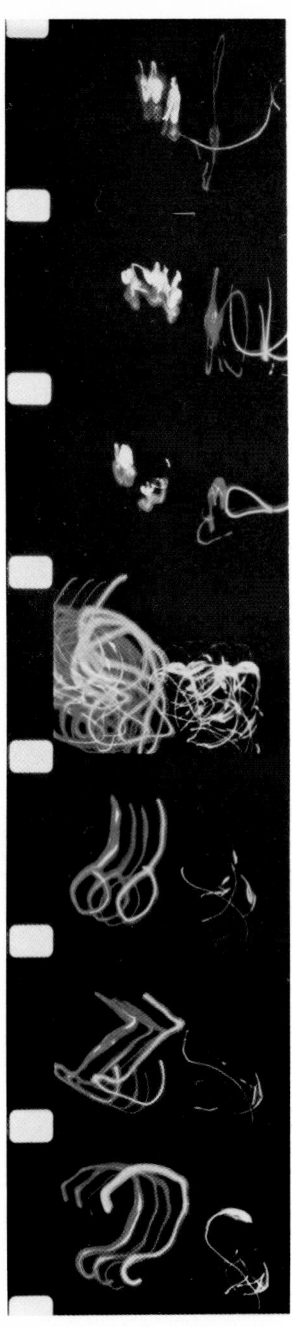

Notebook by Marie Menken

Photo: Francine Keary

The Bed by James Broughton

Soft Rain by Ken Jacobs

Photo: Hollis Melton

The End by Christopher MacLaine

Photo: Hollis Melton

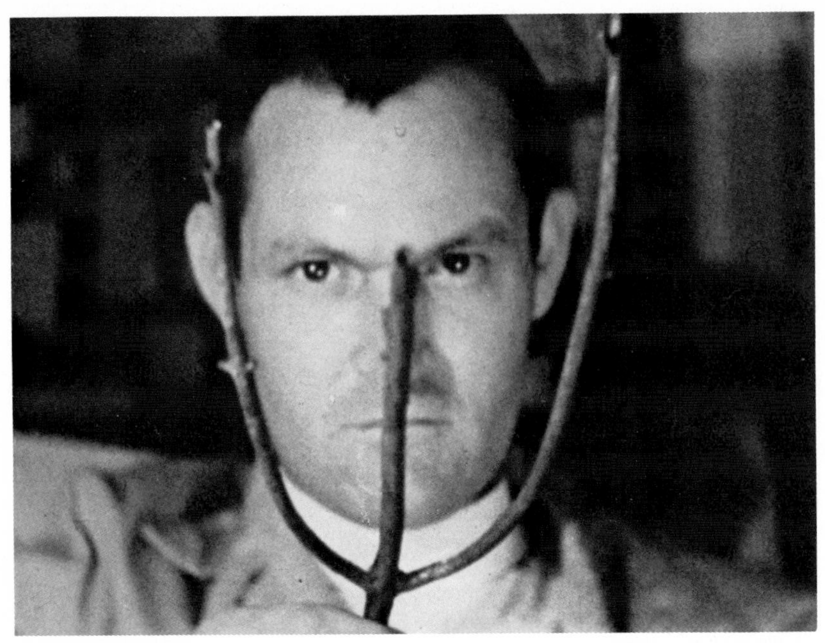

PHOTO: Hollis Melton

The Man Who Invented Gold by Christopher MacLaine

The Petrified Dog by Sidney Peterson PHOTO: William R. Heick

Choreography for Camera by Maya Deren

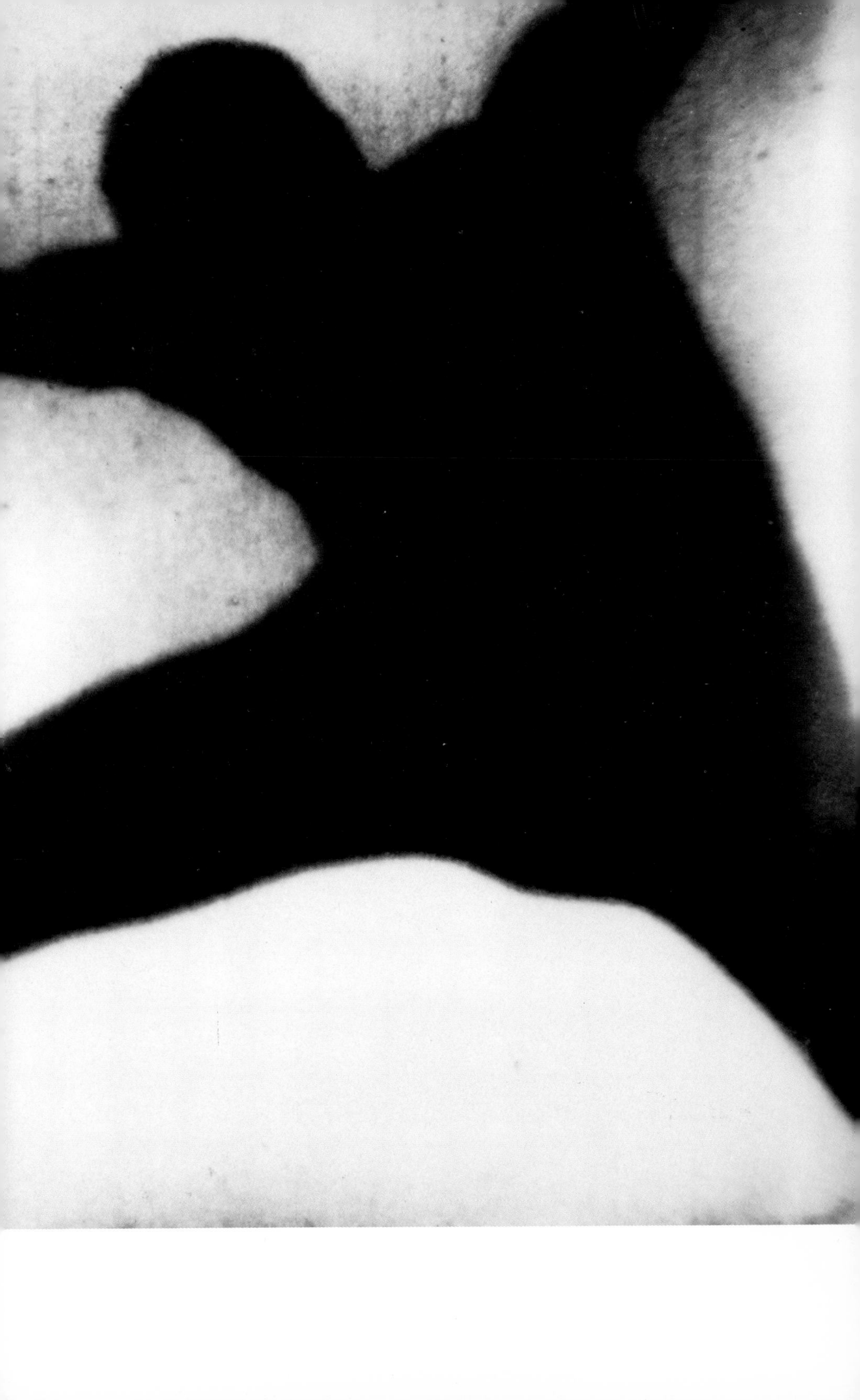

Mother's Day by James Broughton

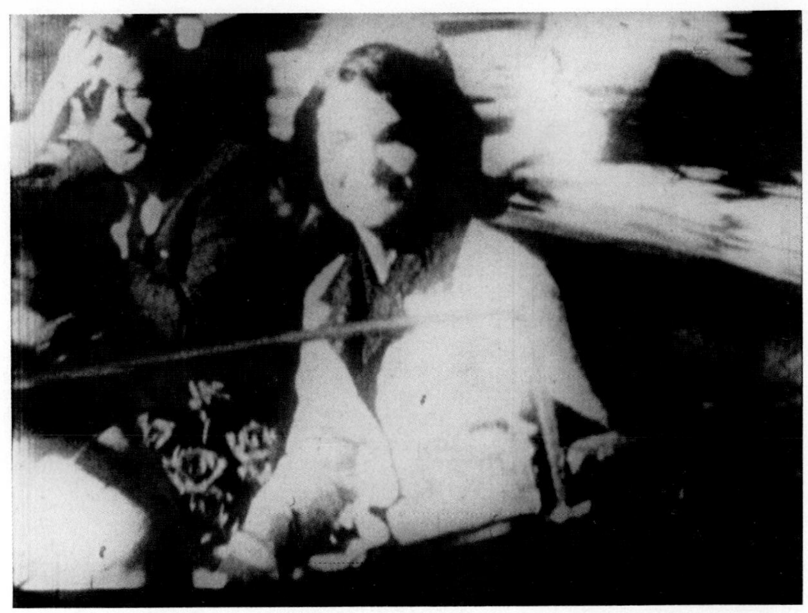

Report by Bruce Conner PHOTO: Hollis Melton

Death in the Forenoon by Jerome Hill

Film Portrait by Jerome Hill

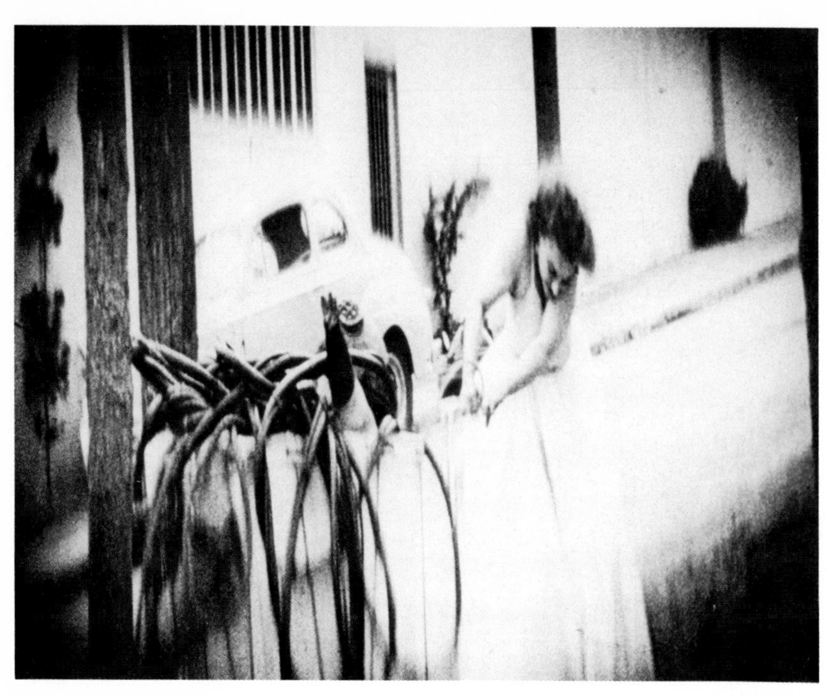

The Lead Shoes by Sidney Peterson

Window by Ken Jacobs

PHOTO: Francine Keary

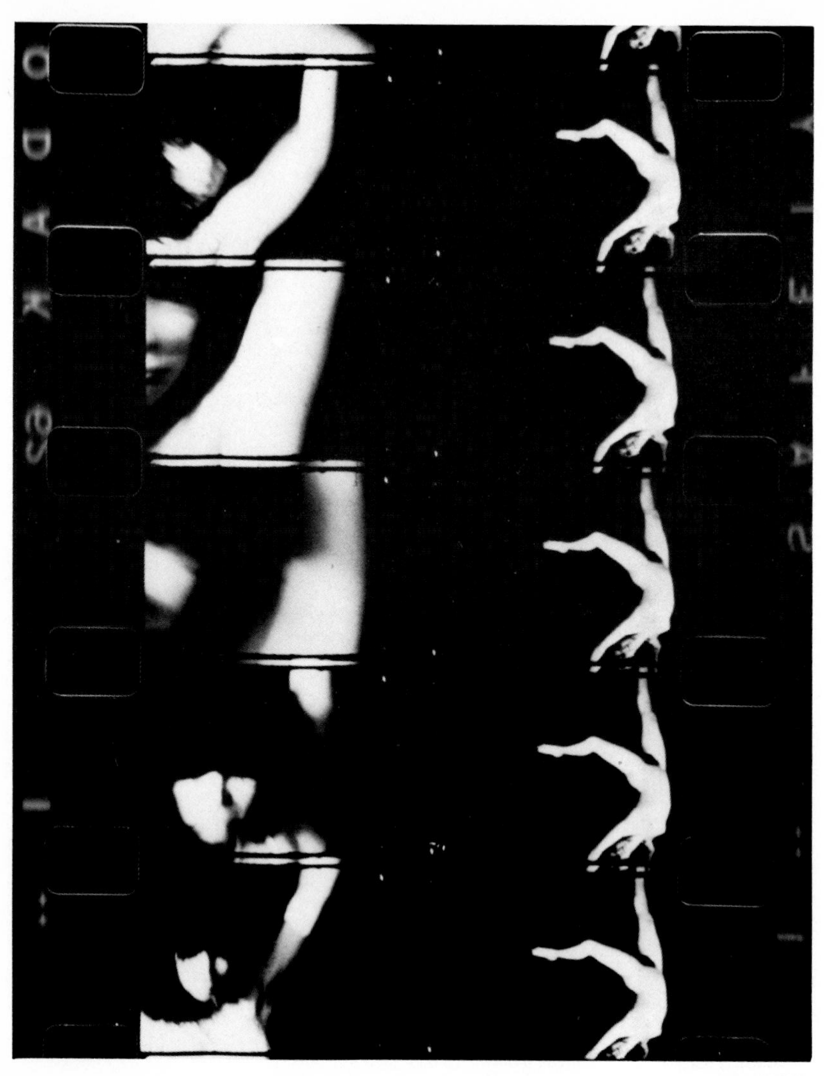

Breakaway by Bruce Conner

of) whose vision was essentially Sasha's — certainly the camerawork and theme. So that once she was off on her own, she was getting attacked everywhere. Wherever there was an out-of-focus shot in her films after she left Sasha, people would say, "Well, it's too bad that they broke up because Maya's such a lousy photographer." But today, we're finally beginning to sense that, far from being a lousy photographer, she was the one with the new vision. And she stumbled into it. The only way, really, to get into new vision is to stumble into it, to start absolutely at the ground.

After "The Private Life of a Cat," Maya and Sasha did not make any more films together. They were living in New York City and pretty much going their own ways. Maya was busy making a reputation for herself as a film artist, no mean trick in those days.

In 1944, she made "At Land," which was utterly free of her quarrel with Sasha. She made it entirely by herself with a camerawoman, Hella Heyman, under her direction. So "At Land" is the first film that is singularly Maya Deren's. It's not been nearly as popular as "Meshes of the Afternoon" for the reason that it's not as simply or as clearly dramatic. But in the long run it is probably going to outlast "Meshes of the Afternoon."

In this period she also began a film, "Witch's Cradle," which was never completed. It was filmed on the occasion of a surrealist show in a gallery. Her concern was to show the charge and the power of perfectly ordinary household objects in relationship to the history of magic. She singled out — and especially respected — the surrealists because she felt that they had created objects of magic from daily household things. Perhaps the only natural heir to this tradition is Claus Oldenberg, whose work Maya would have loved.

Then, also in 1944, Maya tackled dance. She had always been intrigued by dance; in fact, when she had first applied to work for Katherine Dunham, she had had the idea of becoming a dancer. Still, from her association with the Dunham troupe, her intrigue with dance had become quite avid, and she had learned as much as most professional dancers on the subject. Now, while she was hearing, dunned in on her ears daily, that she wasn't a great photographer like Sasha – who was one of the foremost photographers – she *did* know dance. So next came "A Study in Choreography for Camera," which "starred" one of the Dunham dancers, Talley Beatty.

Maya made some fascinating filmic discoveries while she was filming "Choreography," and she made them by accident. She did not know – as Sasha did – at which speed to make a pan so that it would not strobe; and that lack of knowledge resulted in one of the exciting things about this film. When she pans across the trees in the beginning, they "strobe" because she was shooting at the wrong speed. The effect is magical: as it says in the poem, "the little hills do leap," so the trees *do* leap. They are in a state of dance, and provide right at the beginning a moving, leaping, purely visual counterbeat to the smoothness that this human body of Talley Beatty could accomplish.

She used a multiple number of camera speeds in filming "Choreography." It should be the most noticeable thing about the film, although I myself had to see it a number of times before I recognized it – or that this is the real strength of her work. In Beatty's opening scene, he moves more slowly than he appears to do in some of the later slow-motion scenes. But this opening scene was shot at normal camera speed. Even though he had marvelous control over his body, he could not move as smoothly as a slow-motion shot would make him appear: he moves with jerks, and these jerks and slight movements are so fragile and of such a delicacy, that they rhyme with all the little branches of the trees around him. So that he *is* a rhyme with the trees. In fact, during the first pan across, he can almost be missed as being a tree.

If Beatty had done a fast motion in that scene and Maya had filmed it in slow-motion, the movement would have come off very smoothly, without the tremblings of his fingers and his muscles. But as she filmed it, the slight little shifts of his muscles really show.

And this is something film can do for dance; because unless you're sitting where no one sits at the ballet — in the first few rows of the theater — you'll never see this kind of fragile muscular trembling. But in the movies you cannot conceal this; if you're truly going to have a slow-motion and smooth, slow movement, it must be accomplished via the camera.

At other points, Maya's camera makes Beatty seem to do what not even Nijinsky could do: he hangs in air. And in another shot, she photographed his movements in reverse, so that we see a leap that is physically impossible, yet possible in film.

This little tiny film is filled with things whose power we can only see if we're really looking; and all of Maya's work, to some extent, has this quality. By this time Maya had achieved a perfection in her filmmaking style.

In "At Land," for instance, she crawls down the rocks in a particularly stylized way. The body is twisting like a dancer's — she's doing a dance, a very stylized dance movement. In parts, we see her in a sensuous relationship with those rocks; then in the next shot she goes down to the beach like a little girl, in a quite "realistic" movement. Throughout her works she uses this juxtaposition of highly stylized with "realistic" or naturalistic movements. Maya's varieties of movements — both as a photographer and as an "actress" — each with its variety of meaning, can be seen in all her films, such as "Ritual in Transfigured Time" and most especially "Meditation on Violence." For myself, this is a film that I least understood at the time I first saw it; and it was most attacked at that time. But now it seems to me on an absolute equality with "A Study in Choreography for Camera."

The next thing that happens in Maya's life is that she applies for a Guggenheim grant, to go to Haiti; at first, only in order to make a living, to have some project that she thinks might be acceptable to get her some way to go on financially for another few years. She received it, to travel to Haiti and make photographs of the Haitian dances. It was as a person who had toyed with dance and made a dance film that she went, and the Haitian Voodoun dances were the ones that had most intrigued her ever since her days with the Katherine Dunham troupe. So she set off for Haiti, planning to be there for only a few months. She stayed for eighteen, during which period she became the only white woman ever to be taken into Haitian Voodoun ritual; that is, she was entirely accepted by the inner circle of Voodoun, and she became a Voodoun priestess in the highest sense possible.

She returned with thousands of feet of film, and in the course of the next two and a half years, raised more money and went back to Haiti and photographed again and again. And she began to write *Divine Horsemen*, which subsequently became the most highly regarded anthropological document on Haitian Voodoun ritual. During the writing of the book, Maya finally came to peace with her father (who had died in 1943, four years before she first left for Haiti). She knew that he would have approved of this book. But equally significant for her was the fact that, in becoming adopted into the inner circles of Voodoun, she had beat out an even more patriarchal society than the one she was born and reared in.

But there is an interesting mystical conclusion to Maya's Haitian film. She sat on what was finally twenty-five or thirty thousand feet of color film of the Voodoun rituals and never could bring herself to edit that footage into a final form. It overwhelmed her.

When she came back to New York, Maya became the priestess of a Voodoun cult in the city, which was very extensive and, I assume, still is. I myself saw magic and rituals practised that make any Hollywood treatment, like "Rosemary's Baby," seem pale and pathetic by comparison.

It so happened that, due to a concatenation of events in my own life (mostly financial), I came to be staying at her apartment for several months, on one of the four or five couches in her living room. This was the famous apartment on Morton Street in Greenwich Village. There was never a time when I was there that people weren't sleeping on at least two of those couches – an itinerant jazz musician, or maybe someone just over from Haiti, or another artist down on his or her luck . . .

The place was an extraordinary apartment. It consisted of the entire top floor in an older apartment house. As well as the array of couches, the living room had a fireplace whose mantle held large bottles of rum with very disturbing looking roots in them – they looked like the trapped souls of something or other, twisty and gnarly – special imports of things from Haiti. The walls were covered with Haitian Voodoun ritual objects and a United Nations of art work – Chinese, Japanese, European – a desperate struggle to resolve whatever opposites might be in the air. But the primary artifacts of the apartment were certainly Voodoun and consisted primarily of drums – small drums and huge drums. Almost every other night, on the average, there would be a gathering at her apartment, either spontaneous or by serious appointment through the inner Voodoun circles of the city. And rituals would be performed, the very least of which would be some dance to celebrate something or other, and the most of which would involve spreading chalk patterns across the whole floor, in some cases around a nude ill person who was being treated for some disease or possession.

Off to one side, just inside the front door, was a tiny little room, separated from the rest of the apartment by chicken wire. Maya, you see, had cats, some of whom did not get along with each other. In fact, one of the ironies that she loved so much was that the Siamese cat behind the chicken wire, named Erzulie after the Haitian goddess of love, was so desperate a bitch that she fought with everything that came near her. I particularly remember her other cat, named in honor of Ghede, the Haitian god of death and life, as the most enormous cat I ever saw in my life – it was like a small mountain lion. These two cats, Ghede and Erzulie – Death and Love – used to parade back and forth on either side of the chicken wire shrieking the worst feline obscenities at each other. And once in a while one would get where the other one was, and it was an incredible ball of whirling fur and claws. Every three or four days, it seemed, a fight had to be stopped, and I always seemed to be the one to have to stop it.

Maya herself possessed a rare intensity. She had a powerful inner strength, which often terrified men, literally terrified *most* men. I've seen big brawny men — Irish writers or someone just out of the pen — arrive at Maya's and become like terrified small children, reduced to just yes-ma'am, no-ma'am. Not only because she was fierce, but because she was also incredibly sexy. Ah! Just to shake hands with her was arousing!

She was also a fabulously sensuous dancer. When the drums got going, she would dance, at times dancing herself into a genuine trance.

So it was dancing and chalk and cats fighting day and night. And Maya working, typing furious letters, to the *Village Voice*, to Dan Eastman, to the president of the United States, to the Museum of Modern Art, lamenting and carrying on about the needs of people. Because that was always, finally, her central concern — the needs of people. I never saw anyone who came to her house in a threadbare coat on a cold night who didn't get a warmer coat to wear away from it; I never saw anyone come to her house hungry who didn't leave with a good meal in his stomach. I never saw anyone come there who just *looked like* he or she needed a place to stay for the night who wasn't offered a couch. And of course, you often didn't sleep on those couches at night, what with the drumming and the dancing. And how in the world she ever got away with it, I never knew. Perhaps it was that there was such an aura about the place, people just never asked questions. Perhaps her downstairs neighbors had come up once, saw something and never came back.

By this time, Voodoun was very much a center of Maya's life, and she never tried to hide it a bit. Here, for instance, is a party invitation which she sent to friends. It was for a Hallowe'en party, to be held Saturday, October 31, 1959:

A Party in Honor of Ghede

> Ghede, alias Osiris, Dionysus, Shiva, etc., is the Haitian god of the underworld, lord of the dead, keeper of the cemeteries, as archivist of all man's knowledge of experience from the beginning of time. He is the wisest of the gods, and the one who eats and eats and eats, consuming the universe. In Haiti, the weekend of October 31st is dedicated to him, while here in the US the apples bobbing in the tub of water are quite probably the earth, moon and sun floating in the firmament with the hungry gaping mouth hovering over them to consume them. And who ate up the guts of the pumpkin, leaving us a burnt-out, hollow, orange shell of a sun in which we put a candle, hoping by sympathetic magic to keep the sun going, however dimly, through the winter months. But Ghede is also the god of life, of the eternal erotic in man which insures life's continuity apart from the elations and despairs, the will and reason of man, and so Ghede is also the force which feeds life back into the world and keeps the cycle turning. He is also guardian of the children, and on this one night of the year, he takes precedence over all parents, and they go out in his name in skeletons asking for food, doing mischief, upsetting all things. . . . Trick or treat means feed me or I'll upset everything. The clown, the joker, the king's fool, etc. does not respect the king himself. As sovereign of the underworld he is the Master Magician. In his honor we will have a magic show performed by Charles Reynolds, also known as an editor of *Popular Photography*. Please forgive the lateness of the invitation . . . and please come.

About the time that I was staying at the Morton Street apartment, a close friend of hers, the dancer Jeffrey Holder decided to get married. He was a beautiful, tall Haitian who, earlier that season, had danced in "Aida" at the Metropolitan Opera – a special dance that had been created for him. At this time he was starring in "The Flower Drum Song," and he and his leading lady decided to marry. So this was hot stuff. The Broadway people behind the production stepped in and decided to make an occasion of the wedding – to make a publicity event out of it for the show. So they selected a house on Long Island for a gala reception and invited all the Broadway notables as well as a few battalions from the press. Jeffrey agreed to all this, with one condition: that Maya Deren would be in charge of the Voodoun wedding rituals.

Maya was delighted by the idea, and asked Larry Jordan and myself to go and do the photography. Larry and I arrived at the house that Sunday afternoon, to find that Maya was furious. She had managed to put up some ceremonial lanterns and masks, but then the producers of this event had insulted her — they had refused to let her put up certain other ritual objects and had treated her rather with contempt. Well, she did look like the wildest woman on earth to those professional Broadway people — who work so hard at being strange that when they encounter any genuine human strangeness, it gets their backs up. So they had relegated her to a back room, and she was very unhappy. Still, she asked if Larry and I would take pictures of the beautiful Haitian lanterns and masks that she had got up before she had been pushed aside.

The guests and the press arrived with much ado and flash-bulbs, and the party got going. People were chit-chatting around the bar and a huge dining table filled with fancy hors d'oeuvres. Then, suddenly, in the middle of this jammed New York cocktail-party atmosphere came blood-curdling screams from the kitchen. All the help came running from that direction, yelling at the tops of their lungs and elbowing their way through this crowd of sophisticates to get out the door and out of there. Then came the sounds of crashes from the kitchen.

I got to the kitchen in time to see Maya Deren, growling and possessed and in a terrific rage, pick up a refrigerator and hurl it from one corner of the kitchen to another. This wasn't a little luncheon icebox — it was a standard-sized kitchen refrigerator. I could not believe it. I was standing there, frozen to the spot, watching her hurl that thing about four feet across the room — and then everything else in the kitchen started flying. Watermelons went careening out the door, pots and pans, china — she was throwing everything.

The other people in the house were calling for the police by then. But Holder rushed in and threw a protection around Maya. A group of Haitians formed a ring around her and said not to call for the police, that they would handle this themselves. And so they began to calm her down according to the rituals of the religion. She left the room, still growling, and was taken upstairs. As it was explained to me, she was possessed by Papa-Loco, the Haitian god of ritual, tradition and artists.

Some time later, I was called to the upstairs room. One of the Haitians came and said, "Maya wants you." I was, frankly, terrified. But I went upstairs, and as I stepped inside the room, two men grabbed me by the arms and held me. Maya was sitting on the bed with her hair standing completely on end, and she was growling, "MMMMGRAAHN," over and over again. If I hadn't been held, I surely wouldn't have stuck around there very long.

Next, as best I can remember, someone came up with a bowl of blue burning liquid and spooned it out all over the front of my suit. All I could do was to look down and see my suit burning from lapel to cuff, and all I could think was that this was my only suit and it was on fire. I started brushing it out frantically before it died out on its own.

Then some words were said in a voice that I cannot imagine as Maya's. This is the power of Haitian Voodoun: that the voice, the manner, the whole person becomes so different, that you almost see the god that's in possession. At the end of this blood-chilling chant, I was informed that I had been blessed by Papa-Loco for having given homage in my art to the Haitian Voodoun ritual and the ritual wedding objects.

After that experience, I wasn't so inclined to doubt the power of Voodoun, or Maya's status in it.

But along the course of her involvement, she became convinced that our society was in great need of rituals. I remember her saying to me, for instance, that the reason we have so many juvenile delinquents (as "youthful offenders" were then known) is that in America there are no rituals of initiation into adulthood. Initiation rituals, she said, always involve breaking through a barrier, and in America the only barrier that is left to a young person to break through is the law. So her concern began to be with ritual, and it is that concern which can be seen in many of her films. I would recommend her film "Meditation on Violence" as one which shows this concern very clearly.

By the time of the Holder wedding, Maya had fallen very much in love with Teiji Ito, who was to become her third husband. They met under peculiar circumstances. One night, she had gone to a movie, and when she left the theater, realizing that she had left her purse inside, she went back looking for it. In the empty theater, she found a fifteen-year-old Japanese boy sleeping under the seats. He was Teiji Ito. She was quite shocked to learn that the theater was his home: he would wait until the place was cleared out, then he would go to sleep. Mornings, he would get up and leave, walking the streets, panhandling. Teiji had run away from a well-off but oppressive family, to be a musician. He had no training, however; he hadn't even had enough public-school education to qualify him for a music course at a junior high school level. But he had a natural talent, which Maya took on herself to bring out.

Maya, in her thirties then, took him in and fell in love with him. They lived together for many years, and were beautiful lovers. They began listening to music together. They would listen to Mozart, for instance, then to Haitian Voodoun music, and Teiji came to realize from the music of these various cultures certain possibilities which he could integrate into a style that would become uniquely his. It is Teiji's music which was put on "At Land" after the film had run silently for many years. He both composed and performed the score.

Teiji and Maya were married, finally, about a year before her death.

Maya's last film project, released in 1959, was "The Very Eye of Night." It was financed by John Latouche, whom she had met when she was with Katherine Dunham in California. Latouche had been the lyricist for some of Dunham's productions, and had since become famous for his work with musicals, including "The Golden Apples." He had also become financially comfortable and wanted to help some of his artist friends. Maya was among them. He agreed to sponsor "The Very Eye of Night."

It took Maya years to complete this film, and the money went way beyond what Latouche felt he could afford. At some point, he cut off the funds. Now, the Deren legend has it that Maya became outraged that Latouche would cut her off, and so she put a curse on him. It is said that Maya had gotten into the practise of putting Voodoun curses on people who displeased her in one way or another. At least she believed that she possessed this power. That is the story, anyway. But in the laws of magic and Voodoun, certain principles operate. An important one is that if one becomes possessed by a god, the gods are responsible for whatever action ensues, provided the possession occurs despite one's personal feelings. But if one ever forces this magic for one's own personal reasons, the gods are blasphemed and may retaliate.

The fact is that Latouche died of a heart attack shortly after Maya is said to have put a curse on him. And, so it is also said, Latouche had friends in a rival group of magicians who operated a curse against Maya Deren, stating when she would die. Maya Deren did die on a Friday, the thirteenth of October, 1961, at the age of 44.

It's not surprising that a legend has grown up around the circumstances of her death, too. Now, Maya had always had money problems, and by 1961, she and Teiji were in debt to just about everyone. It happened then, that Teiji's father died, and Teiji was left a considerable amount — enough, anyway, so that they could get out from under. Maya and Teiji traveled up to New England to collect his inheritance. But they arrived to a frigid reception from his family, who said that they would block his inheritance in the courts as long as he remained married to this much older woman, this "madwoman." Maya, so it is said, went into a fit at this bad news, a fit which has been described in all senses similar to the one I witnessed on Long Island. But it was a forced possession; she lost her temper and tried to curse Teiji's family for purely selfish reasons — the most dangerous thing she could have done, according to the laws of Voodoun. It was her last fit. She had a stroke, a cerebral hemorrhage, and after two weeks in a coma in hospital, she died. It is said that the time she died was 3:13 in the morning.

However much truth there is to the extreme parts of the Deren legend, it is certainly true that Maya was a force — as a personality and as an artist. She was a woman who, without being possessed by Ghede or Loco or any other Voodoun god, could just throw a fit that was beyond anything imaginable. The dynamics and power of the woman herself were overwhelming. I remember an occasion when she was having a show in New York, and the filmmaker Stan Vanderbeek showed up — a young filmmaker at that time. As was his usual in those days, he came wearing his shabby turtleneck sweater and was a little unshaven. Maya went into a violent fit of anger and screamed at this shy, unassuming young man, "How dare you come to my public showing dressed and looking like this! It's an insult to me!" Vanderbeek fled in terror.

I am totally convinced that Maya Deren was at times completely possessed by some incredible force. Whether it was a Voodoun god or something else, it could turn her into a gross, unbelievably deep-voiced and terrifying figure able to perform acts of strength which under normal circumstances would have been beyond her. The stories about her possessions can be explained by psychiatrists, no doubt, as "manifestations of supreme human will under aggravated emotional states," and so on. But not if you're in the face of them.

Yet, her films are so cool; and that's not fashionable in movies these days unless you're talking minimalism. But Maya's films are not minimalistic. They're very complicated, but they come off very simply. Maya knew — as is fashionable to forget these days — that to make a film appear simple is a complicated matter. It's a matter of the complexity of seeing a person whole, or an object whole — of seeing that there are all the contradictions of the universe in any creature, any thing. And yet, that finally, when we truly embrace such complexity, we're back to the simple again.

Today it seems that there's some rift in the lute of the times which makes it hard for people to understand what a solid container you need to hold the kind of complexity as Maya has in her films.

Maya's intrinsic intellectual involvement in film had to do with space and time. This is what she wrote and talked most about — space and time. She wrote, for example:

> There are many uniquely filmic time-space relationships which can be achieved. I can point at random to a sequence from . . . "At Land." A girl enters and crosses the frame at a diagonal. She disappears behind a sand dune in the foreground at the edge of the frame, and the camera at this moment actually stops operating. The girl walks away a considerable distance and takes her place behind a further dune away. The camera then resumes its shooting, and immediately begins to turn in a panoramic movement in the direction in which the girl just left the frame. Since it starts registering at the identical position at which it stopped some five seconds before, there is no spatial indication of the time which has transpired. . . . and so the alienation of the girl from the camera exceeds the actual time which would have presumably been necessary. In this case, a continuity of space has integrated periods of time which were not, in reality, in such immediate relationship. . . .

The era in which Maya worked could almost be characterized by artists, particularly film artists, talking about horizontals and verticals. Maya's discussions would be "The Vertical Montage," by which she meant that film had the possibility of producing an art that existed on many levels – that you did not just run along a narrative line, which she called "horizontal."

Just to tell a story would be using only the horizontal. Maya said that what we need is the vertical as well; that while you have a horizontal, or narrative line, you also have all the depth of it, almost like a cross section. She was always thinking of how to bring out the multiple layers of meaning of everything that went into her films. If Maya made a pan or a tilt, she did so for reasons that have to do, not with the usual way we think of space or of composition in film, but with time and space – to accomplish something with space and time at once.

One gets the sense, in "At Land," when she is crawling along that table, of "the little girl." One can imagine her father's table of Russian intellectuals and academics talking and talking in a formal dinner atmosphere, and here comes the little girl peering over the edge of the table. And how can any child reconcile the world that he or she lives in, which is literally so much closer to the earth and filled with feeling and inpourings of the senses, with the formality, the detachment, of the adult world? One can imagine that, as a child, the little Eleanora Derenkowski might have peered over that table and dreamed of crawling along the edge of it toward her father – of having everyone pay attention to her, thereby to themselves as animal creatures.

It's the animality, the earthiness, of images that strikes one in "At Land." But rather than simply doing some superficial back-to-nature movie, Maya's drive was to walk right into the dragon's mouth.

All her films are filled with such incredible formal situations. In "At Land" she is walking along the path talking to a man. A thousand times she walked along paths talking to a man. The path she chose in this sequence was chosen with care: it's a defined path, with two ruts in it which make two clearly distinct lines, but it is not paved. It is an earthen path, and yet it is distinctly formal. The camera moves with the walkers and pans back and forth between her and the man. And the man becomes many different men. The first time the camera pans over, we see one man, then it pans back to Maya. Then it pans over again, and it is another man. (As a matter of fact, that second man was her friend the film critic and poet Parker Tyler.) Then it passes back to her. This time, when it passes over to the man, it is yet another man (the young John Cage, in fact). And again, to Maya. And again to the man, a fourth man (Sasha Hammid).

So the camera is moving as an eater of space, or a representation of space, and it is leaping in time. And the effect is that this is an amalgam of many walks, many men.

She uses these qualities in her films with such a naturalness, that much can almost pass unnoticed. How many people see that trick photography was involved in the sand-dune sequence in "At Land"? For myself, I was not aware of the leaps in space the first several times I saw the film. Not aware consciously, that is, although the unconscious mind is bound to be shocked and thrilled. And Maya, of course, was always working in the direction of the unconscious mind.

She was a unique artist, and uniquely influential. It is sad that her life took such a turn that she became unable to make more of these fabulous films. Something happened to Maya in Haiti which has happened to a lot of artists in every century. She became deeply and personally involved in a religion and, essentially, that religion destroyed her as an artist. It was a slow, losing, torturesome battle for her, which people watched in great consternation. She became more and more involved in the Voodoun rituals and the drums and the dancing, and more and more desperately tried to justify her works as an embodiment of these religious principles. It became harder and harder for her to make any kind of film, or to complete the Haitian dance film.

It began, as she states in the introduction of her book, *Divine Horsemen*, as a project to photograph ritual dances. She accomplished the filming, then found herself unable to deal with that material, because she felt that, whatever way she approached it, the result would be too superficial. She did not believe that the film had captured what really was involved in the mystical experience of this religion. All the time I was staying at her Morton Street apartment, she was struggling with the footage, writing scripts, rewriting them, making diagrams and story boards, trying to get through to where she could deal with the footage; and she never managed, in the ten years after the last of the actual photographing, to make that film.

At different times after her death, the footage was offered to other filmmakers to edit; and everyone refused, including myself. Finally, Teiji Ito, with his third wife, Cherel, finished the film, "Divine Horsemen." He had gone to Haiti himself and further perfected the Haitian drums. It is his music on the soundtrack. Not long after he completed this long work, he died, also at the age of 44.

Christopher MacLaine

When I first saw a film of Chris MacLaine's I was astonished. It was the 1952 world premiere of "The End," one of the earliest presentations of Frank Stauffacher's Art in Cinema series. I saw it quite by accident, but it inspired a major breakthrough in my work — as it did for all filmmakers.

Within a week or two of that premiere, Stauffacher perchance imported to America Jean Isou's "Venom & Eternity," which was the film, in its nine-hour version, that caused the only riot the Cannes Film Festival has ever seen. All we've ever got in this country is the two-hour version of the Isou film, but that in itself is one of the most powerful films I have ever seen. I am not sure it is a work of art so much as it is a powerful film essay. Isou turns pictures upside down, scratches on them arbitrarily and does everything he can think of to spit upon and destroy the film image. Now, MacLaine never did that in "The End," but that film and Isou's "Venom & Eternity" are two works that stand like two sides of a portal through which every film artist is going to have to pass at one time or another.

In its San Francisco premiere, "The End" also caused a riot; well, perhaps "disturbance" is a more accurate description of what happened — San Franciscans were not quick to riot. Earlier, there had been a kind of fuss when Peterson and Broughton first presented "The Potted Psalm." Then, in 1952 came MacLaine's "The End."

MacLaine was known around town and had gained a reputation as San Francisco's Artaud. He worked with a kind of dedication to madness. How intrinsic this was to his behavior can be seen in his films. He used to put it very simply by saying he fell out of a tree at a certain age and everything in his life had gone awry ever since.

What MacLaine did for money, God only knows – begged on the streets, mooched, finally robbed and stole. I use both "robbed" and "stole," because he had both these qualities of a thief. He was always desperate. He sang and read poetry in the bars. He read poetry with jazz when that became popular toward the end of the Beat movement in the late 1950s. He always thought of himself as a poet. His poems, however, were out-spewings of rage and racketiness. His conversation was always more poetic than his poems. But the man had an innate and powerful sense of rhythm, and that was the main strength of his poetry. I don't think that he really wrote poetry; but he tried to be a poet in a way very similar to Artaud, and he failed for similar reasons. I do not know if MacLaine ever thought of himself as "the Artaud of San Francisco," but he certainly did have an affinity with him: he courted madness and he finally got it.

Chris MacLaine was also very much a creature of his milieu. In San Francisco (and in some other cities and times of this culture), you almost had a "gathering of the tribes" with the Beat movement. Something similar happened later with the "Hippie" movement in San Francisco before it, too, became known by the world and was re-enacted on the national stage for the slick magazines and the TV networks on a grand Cecil B. DeMille scale. But this was the early 1950s, when the Beat movement was at its maximum intensity among the tribes that the art circles had formed in the late 1940s in San Francisco. By 1958 the Beat movement was old enough and done-for enough that it became the property of the mass media.

The two men most often considered as the exponents of "Beat" were Allen Ginsberg and Jack Kerouac. Ginsberg had been to San Francisco and had written the great Beat poem "Howl." Jack

Kerouac finally produced the great prose statements of the Beat generation with *The Subterraneans, The Dharma Bums* and *On the Road*. But this was all long after the fact. With MacLaine, we are going back to the source of the Beats; he was the filmmaker who chronicled the movement as it happened and created a center of one of the aspects of the Beat myth seven or eight years before the grand epic of "Beat" became nationally known with Ginsberg and Kerouac.

With time, we've come to see that many of the things that the beatniks criticized were not authentic complaints; but one lamentation that holds true is simple, and Chris MacLaine always reminds me of it. His whole generation had just returned from World War II (those who hadn't been killed in it); they had missed their adolescence. They had been taken suddenly and thrown abroad into a war when, in a saner world, a saner time, they would have been enrolling in college or passing through other civilized rites of adolescent passage. Crucial years of their growing-up were missing. This marked the generation that became the center of the Beats.

"The End," as I've said, is MacLaine's first film. After that he made "Beat" and "The Man Who Invented Gold" and, finally, his last completed work, "Scotch Hop." So he began his artistic statement with "The End," a great epic film. It may seem strange to refer to a 45-minute film as epic, but it manages epical as well as introverted perfections. It tackles the atomic bomb — the first handling of it in art, and as a neurosis, that I know of. I have seen the film more than fifty times, and there are moments when I still begin to tremble at the psychological blockages and outright terror of it. Unquestionably, it is MacLaine's masterpiece. It has been voted into the Anthology Film Archives. Anyone who shows Chris MacLaine will show "The End" if nothing else. In addition to being a great work of art, in my opinion, it is one of the most prophetic of our time. It prophesied dozens of major roles that film was to take, both as a medium and as an art; and it also prophesied aesthetic directions and style trends.

Yet, when "The End" first came out in San Francisco, it caused a disturbance, and to some audiences it is still disturbing and even embarrassing. Why? Well, we are very pap-fed, particularly in America. Imagine someone who has eaten only Kraft American cheese and who is handed a piece of limburger. He'll say, "My god! What is this? A piece of shit? All moldy and smelling and coming apart." That is the analogy of anyone who's been fed on Hollywood or TV pap and who sees "The End" or any other MacLaine film for the first time. One must accept MacLaine's "limburger" as a connoisseur would. You give any child who is used to American processed cheese a piece of limburger or bleu cheese, or any American who is used to TV movies a MacLaine film, and he's going to make a face over it — at first, until his palate has been educated to accept new tastes.

It is difficult to have a feeling for new art; it is abrasive because it is new — it hurts in a way, and puts you off. It is abrasive until perhaps one hundred years of people talking it to death have put a pearl sheen on it. This is always the case; and it always has been during the great eras of a culture that people are educated to accept this abrasiveness, to be interested and intrigued by it.

Very often it is the case that what is considered a weakness in one work of art becomes the greatest strength in another, similar work. In all of Chris MacLaine's work, one of the greatest strengths is the self-consciousness of the people he photographs — not only self-consciousness but camera-consciousness. The whole movie industry since the beginning of film has struggled to achieve a nonchalance among actors in front of the camera. Most Hollywood stars are judged by the degree to which they can be indifferent to the camera, to give the appearance that there is no camera photographing them. MacLaine reverses that, and the result is that, as you view his films, you become more and more amazed at the degrees and variety of people's self- and camera-consciousness.

This self-consciousness should not be confused with the self-consciousness of the actors one sees in Jean Cocteau's films who don't act convincingly. For Cocteau, this is a genuine weakness, as he used amateurs along with professional actors. In Chris's work, anyone who does not look self-conscious is the rare exception. The apparent amateurishness of his filmmaking is deliberate; one might say that he went clear out to the end of the amateur limb. And it was exactly this amateurish look which fascinated him. He is always making love to these photographed women with his camera ineffectually, and obviously so. His heroes are always pale, tormented neurotic young men who cannot quite limp down to the beach or even masturbate effectively. Via those emblems, MacLaine symbolized the intrinsic center of the Beat movement.

MacLaine is one of the most difficult of filmmakers to understand. Some would say that that is because he is one of the weaker filmmakers, and that this weakness can be seen in much of his work. There are seeming flaws in his work, and we are still analyzing his films to determine whether they are in fact flaws or whether we simply approach his films with prejudices that make them appear to us flawed. But in any case, Chris MacLaine is an artist. I don't think that anyone who has seen much of his work doubts that.

As one looks at his film "Beat" one sees more of the humor in his camera movements. People are made to walk fast and look jerky in his films, and this is intentional humor; he was not content to shoot at eight frames a second — he skips frames so that people skip ridiculously in a way that rhythmically captures their intrinsic self-centeredness. They parade, like the woman in "Beat." No more perfect metaphor for street life in North Beach at that time could be found than the woman in "Beat" who behaves as though she were free and lovely (with an umbrella — she is Gene Kelly singing in the rain). But she is like a turtle trapped in a cage, going around the four corners of an intersection. One can look at this as humorous or as unbearably horrible. If you can regard it as both delightful and horrifying, you are close to the balance that makes MacLaine an artist. To me, "Beat" evokes that era to a T — beautifully, precisely, wittily and terrifyingly.

I went back to San Francisco in the early 1960s, when the Beat movement, even in its decadent, nationally publicized phase, was dying out; and I was appalled to find that many of the filmmakers who had seemed so important in the early days of the Beat era were almost totally forgotten. They were forgotten for one reason: at that time everything in this country still had to pass through Manhattan Island; and the essence and genuine strengths of the Beat movement (and, later, the Hippie movement) never did get through that needle's eye of the east coast very comfortably.

So Chris MacLaine was forgotten then. Nobody even knew who I was talking about. So I set myself the task of finding him.

I knew the dives I would have to search, and I knew of some people who had known him on and off during the decade of my absence from San Francisco. Finally I found someone who told me to go to such-and-such a real estate company. "Just walk through the office," he said, "and go out the back door, and don't pay any attention to anyone who yells at you. If you go into the courtyard in back and turn left, there are some rickety stairs, and about two thirds of the way up the stairs you'll see a window. Yell in that window, and you'll probably find Chris MacLaine."

These directions were pretty bizarre, but I'd known that I would never find MacLaine by following a straight line, so I went to the realty company and walked in. Immediately, a rather fat and balding man wanted to know what I wanted, and as I walked past him, opening the gate in the counter, he began to shout to at me, "Hey! What are you doing? What do you want?" I kept walking to the back door, with him yelling and screaming behind me that he wasn't going to stand for this anymore. Outside, I found the stairs, and nearly broke my neck on the first three. I tip-toed carefully upward and saw several windows. One of them was open just a bit. It was dirty and cracked, and I peered in and called, "Mr. MacLaine?" No answer.

By now I was beginning to think that maybe I had been put on, and I certainly didn't feel like going back into that real estate office to get out of here. So I started up the steps again. I had just passed the window I had called into when I heard a voice, "What do you want?" I looked down and saw one of the most terrifying faces I had ever seen in my life — mean, stubble-bearded, desperate, eyes rolling, pupils dilated. I told him who I was looking for. He said he was Chris MacLaine and added, "I knew you must be okay wearing those green pants." He opened the window; I climbed down into the room and found that the window truly was the only entrance or exit to MacLaine's domicile.

It was a room filled with bric-a-brac — old door knobs, candlesticks, broken baroque and rococo plaster pieces that had once been carved into ornate shapes. Most of the stuff was metal, all highly polished. If I had known as much about such things then as I know today, I'd have known immediately that Chris was on speed. He had polished every shiny surface in the place to such a sheen that even in the gloom they all glowed almost with lights of their own. He also had a vast collection of knives in the room, all sharpened to razor pitch, from the tiniest pocket knife to the largest of cleavers.

I knew that MacLaine was about 35 to 38 years old, but the man in that room with me looked more like 55. He was a man so reduced in circumstances — materially, spiritually, physically and morally — that I could barely believe I was actually in the presence of one of the filmmaking geniuses of the time. He was desperate in every respect.

He told me that he had not made any films for years. Up to this time, the only MacLaine film I knew of was "The End." But during our conversation, I learned that he had made three other films: "Beat," "The Man Who Invented Gold," and "Scotch Hop."

The lead character in "The Man Who Invented Gold" is Chris MacLaine. The film is an autobiography of his spiritual life, and also a great deal of his social life. The first time you see him in the film, he is holding up a forked stick, and you see a rather chubby

Chris. Then you see him with his Scottish way of wearing his beret, or his tam, bagging down to one side. What is interesting about this film is that Chris had also had other people play him. One of them looks superficially like him hidden behind a beard and glasses; this stand-in is there for ambiguity rather than affinity. Another stand-in was Larry Jordan; and still another one is a man who resembles Jordan. The ambiguity is intentional; and once you recognize the ambiguity, you realize that any one of these men might have been the man who invented gold. And then the film leaves that big "You" thrown back at the audience: Are you the man who invented gold?

The voice in the film is MacLaine's; he was perfectly aware that the voice sounds like an amateur filling in for a narrator; so once again, what would be a weakness in some other artist's work becomes a strength in MacLaine's. There is also the awkwardness of the camera, of the "actors," the substitution of one actor for another in a role — MacLaine transforms all these things into a forte.

The greatest moments in art are often the result of an unforeseen difficulty: there is an accident, or funds are cut off, or something breaks. And then something unsought-for happens. It is the mark of a genius to recognize it and use it, and use it with consistency. In the making of "The Man Who Invented Gold," such a thing happened to Chris. He had somehow persuaded Jordan Belson to be his cameraman. Belson is an extraordinary cinematographer, and the most extremely opposite filmmaker from MacLaine that there is. He is ordinarily incapable of producing the sort of funky, uncomposed, shaky shot that MacLaine is known for; and the two men's temperaments are as opposite each other's as their filmmaking techniques. But somehow, he agreed to do the shooting for MacLaine.

Belson once told me a story of his experience with MacLaine which delighted me because it was so true to Chris's spirit. "One rainy morning," Belson said, "Chris came to my house and just threw the door open without knocking and stood there in shaggy, baggy clothes dripping water on my rug and smelling like a winery. He had a dirty, crumpled, illegibly scrawled-on scrap of paper in his hand, and he threw it at me and said, 'These are your shooting instructions for this afternoon.' "

Well, despite Belson's bent for sticking out a job, at some point MacLaine's utterly chaotic and mad world got the best of him and he quit. It was at that point that MacLaine had to take up the camera himself. So he started finding stand-ins, and out of that necessity he created the wonderful ambiguities in "The Man Who Invented Gold."

During that period when I was back in San Francisco, I made friends with Chris MacLaine as best one might under the circumstances. He was rapidly disintegrating from the effects of speed. In order to support his habit — and his speed-addict's acquisitiveness for sharp knives and shiny objects — he robbed and he stole.

He came to visit us many times, and each visit was difficult. Jane and I had a household full of life, with our children, our pets, and a lot of optimism. Chris was nervous, distraught, seeking his own annihilation. Sometimes it was dangerous to have him in the house at all. Without meaning any harm, he would suddenly throw his arm out in a gesture, oblivious to the fact that the children were nearby and that he might hit them. One day he threw a knife — as impulsively as he made those wide-armed gestures — and it stuck in the wall near where the cat and her kittens were bedded down. I kept telling him that we couldn't have that, or his drug-taking, in our house, and for a while he would agree; and then he'd come back and there would be another crazy incident. Once, for example, he said that our back yard was full of weeds; we agreed that it was, and Chris went out to cut them. He seemed to have one of those sudden enthusiasms of the "speed freak" while he was out there and started cutting down everything — trees, vines, Jane's beloved hollyhocks. There was no stopping him, and I daresay that he would have killed anyone who had tried to stop him — he was that kind of creature, finally. Within an hour, he had destroyed every living thing in the back yard.

Eventually, I had to ask him not to come by anymore.

After many attempts I arranged a meeting for him with a distributor in San Francisco, Willard Morrison, who signed contracts for his films and got them preserved. MacLaine's films have been renting at increasing rates, but Chris cannot benefit from any of the money that has come in; there is a large sum which, I assume, will finally go to the State of California, because they have been taking care of him since about 1965.

I saw Chris by chance in 1968, on the street. At that point he was about 45 years old — he looked an extraordinarily worn 70. By then he had no wits whatever. He could not recognize me or, I am sure, anyone. The state institution where he was living let him go out for walks around the block; he would wander through his old haunts in North Beach, then go back to get his supper and go to bed. He was completely destroyed. And yet he had been a great artist.

In "Scotch Hop," his last completed work, Chris, for perhaps the first and only time in his filmmaking life, dropped all his concern with himself as mad or the world as "The End" or the misery of existence; and he went with his camera to the Convention of San Franciscan Scotsmen and created a very short and very enjoyable film — one which I think is the purest little masterpiece that he ever created.

As is the case with his earlier works, with "Scotch Hop" we have an extraordinary, wonderful expression of adolescence. How many portraits do we have in the arts of that important period in everyone's life? To give a genuine portrait of it, one would almost have to be an adolescent himself. MacLaine was somehow able to hold onto the qualities of adolescence — the awkwardness at the dawn of grace and the embarrassments — yet to remain sure of himself as a filmmaker all the same. So the "embarrassing" qualities that might otherwise be tossed away are what make "Scotch Hop" — and all of his films — so precious. An amateur filmmaker would have been embarrassed by his mistakes and therefore unable to push his errors through to a statement that includes them as characteristics. MacLaine had the courage and greatness, and the madness, to keep his photography throughout his films characteristic.

He was an artist who could weave tapestries from disparate shots so that there is an unbroken continuity of rhythm. This is one of his strengths that can be seen most clearly in "Scotch Hop." The rhythm in that film is fantastic. He has a close-up of a bagpipe player, and the movement of the man's cheek is a major statement of rhythm within the frame; then the image that follows falls into its absolute rhythmical place.

One of the great problems in a visual art is subject matter. You can say of a subject, "This is a little boy trying to throw a little log in imitation of grown men in a log-throwing contest." But to get the little boy in there and to keep his image as a rhythmic piece of the whole — and not to break the continuity — the image of the little boy must be placed with rhythmic grace. That is what MacLaine does. He accomplishes his consummate rhythmic grace with color schemes, as well — editing so that the shots and cuts interrelate. He uses this technique in "Scotch Hop," with very dark shots recurring with consistency in relation to the extremely light shots.

The bagpipes are played with a particular rhythm, according to the breathing of the player. The whole sound experience is filled with a sense of breathing. The drums, then, are played with another sort of rhythm, and the film itself makes a third rhythm. And they all fit each other.

MacLaine did not accomplish the exquisite rhythmic sense of "Scotch Hop" by sitting down and figuring dry tables of numbers and rhythms or studying the formalities of composition and rhythm. Others may talk of the technical details of rhythm — the methods to attain it, its analysis and explanations — but they would not be able to make such a masterpiece as "Scotch Hop." Chris MacLaine was able to accomplish what he did with this film because he loved what he was filming. He had his day — perhaps only one such day in his whole miserable life. He had a camera with him and he had worked with it for years, and he knew how to operate it so that it did not interfere with him. He danced with it.

An artist cannot make a masterpiece unless he has opened himself and loved something enough to get it all the way over to the audience, and MacLaine did this with "Scotch Hop." When you can be open enough to care about other works and other people and other things, and then study techniques enough to know how to use the medium — how this or that film stock performs, where to buy and from whom, which lens gives you this or that effect — and if you keep at it and care enough, and if the gods give an occasion when you have a camera with you and you are full of love and excitement, and the film lab doesn't screw up the film and gets it safely back to you, and then if you have enough enthusiasm left to sit at a dusty table with it and reconstruct that moment — then you get a work of art.

The happiest memory I have of Chris has to do with his love of the bagpipes. He was very concerned with his Scottish self. He identified strongly with Scotland, and he played the bagpipes beautifully (in fact, the bagpipe music in some of his films is his own).

It happens that one night when he was visiting us, he refused to leave. It was one of those nights when we kept wanting to go to bed, but his conversation was so fascinating — if terrifying — that Jane and I could only sit and listen. I remember that he kept attaching the world "ville" to everything. It was "this-ville" and "that-ville," and certainly he had us in "MacLaine-ville" with his stories, each of which led to another.

Finally it had got to be nearly dawn, and Chris insisted on playing the bagpipes — they should be played at dawn, he said. I was horrified. "My god, Chris, you can't do that. People are asleep, you'll wake up everyone and they'll send for the police." But there was no stopping him — as there rarely was — and he cut loose with the bagpipes through one of the front bay windows. Then he paraded through the children's room and woke them up.

The children were delighted. They followed him as the children of Hamlin followed the Pied Piper, out through the living room. It is a memory that has haunted them ever since – they still talk about it.

Now, bagpipes, as everyone knows, produce the loudest music known to humankind. Jane and the children and I were feeling the sound in our very bones and nerve endings. The whole house began to vibrate. The windows were rattling and the walls and ceiling were shaking. Finally I just threw open the windows, and all this sound went out to the street and the courtyard.

Then one of those magical moments happened. Outside, instead of the police as I'd expected, people were pouring into the streets to listen, thrilled and enchanted by the bagpipes. It was a complete success, perhaps Chris's greatest public appearance.

That is the way I like to remember Chris MacLaine, standing there at dawn at the open window with his bagpipe, delighting San Francisco.

Photo: Robert A. Haller

Bruce Conner

Bruce Conner was born in the early 1930s in Wichita, Kansas, and was brought up there through high school, in the same area as I lived in my early childhood, just a few miles from Wichita. He came from the same area as Bob Branneman, the painter and filmmaker, and Michael McClure, the poet. I could go on and on naming filmmakers and poets who were born within a radius of twenty miles in Kansas in the early 1930s — such diverse poets as Ronald Johnson and Ken Irby — all reared in this flat farmland and airplane-building community in and around Wichita; hardly the garden spot of America. It is such an extraordinary phenomenon that one almost wonders what cloud must have formed at this time and touched down in this place to hatch all of these people, most of whom knew or came to know each other.

Most of them went to San Francisco in their late teens, including myself, and met or re-met each other, mainly through the influence of the poet Robert Duncan. I met Michael McClure at Duncan's house, and shortly afterward I met Bruce Conner. He was a "live wire," you might say, in expressing whatever was current in the air and making it last.

Those who had gone to high school together in Wichita had a special kind of relationship — the old "high school cut-ups," happy, smart-ass sharers of a particular esoteric world known only to those who had grown up around Wichita; and they were determined to spring-board into the world — or universe, almost as though the world were too small, which in fact it is beginning to be.

To get a personal understanding of Bruce Conner, or any of these artists, you have to remember where they came from. If you go out into a Kansas cornfield at night and stand there, as they each did, you can hear the music of the spheres; there are no other sounds to hear. I suppose that now jets fly overhead, but even when I was there recently, there was still this incredible silence. People go to bed at 9:00 p.m. and they sleep quietly. There is no wind most of the time. It is flat as far as the eye can see, no clouds in the sky, just this unbelievably hard — and therefore terrifying — blue dome, intensely golden wheat or corn and the violent emerald green of corn stalks level to the horizon, with an occasional freakish tree desperately reaching up.

If you have that sense of the hard blue dome and the impossible silence, no wind and the tremendous summertime heat, then you might begin to know what it meant to Dorothy of L. Frank Baum's *The Wizard of Oz*, or to anyone in Kansas, when the cyclone came. The air goes thin, drops around you, the dome massively gray, and you're wrapped inside a stillness charged with incredible energy. Then suddenly you look and there is something moving like the finger of God back and forth across the horizon, and you ask, is it coming toward you?

So into this dome moves the image of death as the great adventure or as total destruction — or, as Baum makes it in *The Wizard of Oz*, a relief. Will you go up the windspout to the land of Oz and travel to the Emerald City? Some of the little boys and girls in Kansas stand in cornfields and imagine that New York is the Emerald City; many of them go to pieces when they get there. To imagine a city under those circumstances is to imagine a civilization that we do not have.

For so many others, the Emerald City was San Francisco. It was a city that was fun, that was playful, that was beautiful; that people walked in and that was the most civilized. Many of us gravitated there. Conner became very much entrenched; he makes his home there and you will find him very much a part of that bold scene of San Francisco living.

People usually look at Conner's films — as they do at Broughton's — and laugh very superficially, or get a simple delight out of them; but do not take them thoughtfully enough. So I'll start with one of Bruce's films that is difficult not to take thoughtfully, his film on the assassination of President Kennedy, "Report."

"Report" was completed in its first version one year after Kennedy's assassination and shown at a Boston University film class on the anniversary of that awful event. Conner continued to re-edit the film for another year and a half, whenever he made a new print. So there are many 16 mm versions, as well as one 8 mm version.

The 8 mm version was made at the time of the assassination from television images. At that time, Conner was living in Brookline, Massachusetts, just outside of Boston. He went through the catharsis and shock that most of America did. The assassination was so immediate to people; it was on TV, it was on the radio — you could not escape it. Almost immediately, Conner had his camera in hand, and as the television stations started repeating the shots of the assassination, he took images from the television screen, and quickly produced an eight-millimeter film.

This first version is quite different from the film he made several versions of and struggled with for two and a half years. The difference, I think, says a great deal about Conner's work and gives a real perspective on two types of filmmaking. With 8 mm, you have all the immediate potentiality of the powers of a sketch. There is the brevity, the quickness, as well as the light-weightedness of the camera, that expendability of it.

So if film in 8 mm is the sketch, one can say that film in 16 mm is the oil painting, the masterpiece of that sketch. Conner struggled between these two ways — a sketch or a masterpiece — in making the 16 mm version. The 8 mm is the immediate capture of his immediate feelings at the time. The 16 mm is thoroughly worked through.

Of the many versions he made of the 16 mm film, he says that most of the changes were in the first eight minutes. The first eight minutes of the first four editings of this film show certain events repeating and repeating with no variation, such as the one shot which shows the carrying of Oswald's rifle down the hallway. In another version, for eight minutes he repeated, with slight variations, the carrying of the rifle. Then there is the shot of Jacqueline Kennedy going up to the door of the ambulance. I remember this particular shot vividly: the door is locked, and she steps back. In one of Conner's versions, this shot is repeated over and over again. Third, there is the motorcade coming past, before the actual assassination. The fourth is a scene of Jacqueline Kennedy in Washington where the casket is lying in state. She walks up to the casket, kneels down, kisses it and walks away. At the point where she starts toward the casket, the shot is repeated again and again so that she never gets to the casket, just as in the earlier scene, she never gets inside the ambulance.

So there are metaphors on death, intrinsic not only to the Kennedy assassination but, through Conner's use of that occasion, to a very "Kansas" way of facing death.

In watching "Report" in its 8 mm version, many, including myself, have had the feeling of peril and terror when Oswald is going down the hall — although we all know that Ruby steps out at some moment and shoots him almost with the purity of Greek drama. All of us are familiar with those faces and images and what happens, but in Bruce's filming of it, the sense of peril and of terror are still intense. These images shown out of focus and utterly abstract would be nerve-wracking. But suddenly, in their collage effect, they become menacing — a carrier of death; not just the faces of one or two men, but in the wand that seems to come out of the air from the side. This wand is also in the 16 mm version, but it is particularly alive in the 8 mm. There is a movement over on the right as Oswald becomes flanked by two men; and it is as though he were going to be downed by the bad fairy or something. This wand will come down and kill him – or something will – this menacing shark-shape. Or the woman doing the TV commercial, whom Conner "freezes" just as her teeth are bared.

Bruce was just alive and wracked on that day of the assassination, and he had to make his homage. To what? To Kennedy? To Death? Alive and in a state of nervousness before that TV set, he took images charged with the immediacy of the actual event. It should be as real as if you were there: and here sits the artist, and he knows it is not real at all. It is made up of thus and so, and he with his camera is making it up again, trying to get at this event in stark terror and death. This is the quality that makes this film great.

In an interview with *Film Comment* magazine, Bruce was asked if he knew what he was doing when he made "Report." He answered:

> Yes, I knew what I was doing. I was obsessed. . . . I was living in Brookline, Massachusetts, which was the birthplace of President Kennedy. He had reserved a plot in the graveyard of Brookline to be buried in. . . . He was assassinated. I lived seven blocks from where he was born. I decided then to dedicate myself to recording what had happened and what had happened here in Brookline, because he was going to be buried there, and I lived there for the next two or three years to work on that film and make a pilgrimage every day to the grave. Then they took him away from me.

What he refers to here, of course, is that Kennedy was not buried in Brookline, but in Arlington.

On Kennedy's birthday, which was about five months after the assassination, at the hour and minute of his birth, Conner went to the house where Kennedy was born and stood in front of it. On the way he had been listening to the radio: "Today we are putting out commemorative stamps of John Kennedy." Everybody knew that it was his birthday. Hundreds of people went to the grave in Arlington. Hundreds gathered at the assassination site in Dallas. But Conner was the only person standing in front of the house in Brookline, Massachusetts, at that moment. He was the only one there, in a community that knew Kennedy personally. There is something deeply touching in this image.

When Bruce started work on the film in 16 mm, the big problem was that he had to show what happened — the exploitation of a man's death. Again, from Conner's *Film Comment* interview:

> The problem in making the film was that in order for me to do the film I would also have to go through the same processes that these people were using to exploit Kennedy. If the film was completed, then he was as dead as they had made him. So it took me two and a half years to finish the film. That has something to do with why it changed. Part of the reason why it changed, why we go through these eight versions of the 16 mm film, was that I did not want to stop the changes. Like life is change. Like when "Report" was finished — then he was dead. So it took me two and a half years to acknowledge that he was dead.

Much of Conner's work deals with images taken by men who were covering the event — journalists. Conner had decided that, as he had received a Ford Foundation grant, he could purchase stock footage from the electronic news media of some of the same shots he had originally photographed from TV. He purchased them in 16 mm and began working.

Conner buys much of the photography he uses in his films. He photographs off of TV, or he tries to purchase 16 mm footage if he feels that that there is something he can do with the images. I surmise that he has a sense of using everything. This might come from that sort of pioneer frugality of Kansas that wants to make a use of everything. I think that Bruce just hates to throw anything away. If he buys a piece of footage, it bothers him until he finds a place for it. He had quite a stock library. Once someone gave him literally thousands of feet of prints as a gift because it was well known that he would use it all some day, some way. In fact, it tormented him awfully, and he became desperate to get rid of that huge gift. He sent some of it to me. I am sure he kept some of it, waiting to find a place for it.

Repetition, as in "Report," is among the characteristic marks of Conner's films. Yet, he proves that there is no such thing as repetition, in the sense that Gertrude Stein made clear in her book *Making of Americans*. She demonstrates that when you "repeat" a thing, you charge it with another level of energy; so that if you vary it, however slightly, it is dynamic. It is much more dramatic if you repeat an image and make slight variations. Conner repeats, speeds up, then interrupts a shot at a different place each time — a little earlier or a little later, or in a different section of the shot.

He is also very anxious that you see the splice and that you see whatever the mechanics are of putting two pieces together. There is one film, however, in which he makes an exception to this, "The White Rose." Most people have overlooked this film in his work, but I think it is one of his greatest, if not the greatest. In it, he deliberately worked with "A" and "B" roll printing, used to conceal the splices. Every other shot is on a different roll — "checkerboard editing," as it is also called. He went a long way to have no splices showing; thus if we do see a splice, we know he meant it to be seen. If he did not want them seen, he would have hidden them.

I know Bruce was as upset as anyone else about splicing cement. It is very difficult to make a splice nowadays. The reason is that around 1970 Eastman Kodak changed its film base to pure plastic. It no longer had any cotton in it, as the old film base did, and they did not invent a splicing fluid that would effectively hold the plastic together. All over the country many splices made correctly and well with this new pure plastic base started popping apart in the cans after about two years. It is just a simple horrible truth that they have, in fact, created a film base that is essentially unspliceable with any of today's splicing materials. You cannot make it hold together for more than two years; and I am sure that this has driven Conner to despair, as it has me. In fact, I started making films with great long shots primarily for this reason. Conner, who makes many short reprinted cuts, must have been driven completely crazy.

Some more background on Bruce: He became famous, first of all, as a sculptor, and very famous indeed. At the time his fame started to build, he was in Mexico. He and his wife, Jean, moved there. "We went to Mexico," Conner says, "because I had made the most money I had ever made before (or since) in one year from the sales of my art work. Left Mexico at the end with 30 dollars and a car full of art work to head for the border and poverty and the Cuban missile crisis."

While he was there, he sent me a picture he had taken, of a highway with the letters L O V E written in very clearly marked lines across it. I was delighted. I thought, what's happening in Mexico, that they're writing "love" on their highways. It was written so perfectly, that I thought it must have been painted there by the highway engineering department. I learned that a few days later the officials caught Conner writing on another highway and made him take it off. It took him two or three days to scrub it clean.

In the States again, Bruce was "taken up" by one of the galleries in New York; he signed a contract with them. I do not know the specific terms of that contract, but I will say that I have seen contracts for painters with prominent New York galleries that state such things as, "You may not leave the city of New York or its environs for more than two months of every year for the next seven years"; or, "You may not have a publicly acknowledged marriage within the next seven years" or, "You may not change your painting style or exhibit it publicly for the next seven years." I read one contract that had been given to a woman artist to sign which read, "You may not have a publicly recognized child within the next seven years."

As Bruce told me, his contract did have a stipulation that he must attend a certain number of public parties or meetings, as designated by the gallery, every year for the next so many years. The contract might have said such a thing as, "You be at Mrs. So-and-so's house on such-and-such a date," and he would have to be there or have a written doctor's excuse to keep the contract valid. I do not know what the other specific restrictions were, but I do know that they were severe enough to take so beautiful a man as Bruce Conner and leave him with ulcerative colitis within two or three years — desperate ulcers. When I saw him nearing the end of three years under that contract, he could not stop shaking. He shook almost continually. He was so nervous in such a peculiar way that I thought he must be under some strange new drug. But not so. Whatever drugs he may have been taking were just to calm his nerves.

While he was under contract, he was given "benefits" as though he were a stud horse or a football or boxing star. Magazine ads were bought for him; he was "sold" to the American public sufficiently so that museums all around the country bought his sculptures. He was sold exactly like that; and after the contract ended, nothing of his was sold to any museum anywhere. I remember that in the early 1970s, well after this period, I was in Chicago, and wondering if the sculpture which the Art Institute had bought was still there. It was called "Tick-Tock Jelly Clock Cosmotron." When I called to ask Bruce about it, he said, "It's probably there — but down in the basement." I checked, and was happy to see that it was still on exhibit.

Most of the major museums in the country have at least one Bruce Conner sculpture; and most of the books that deal with the newer sculpture will show at least one photograph of a sculpture of his. It all came out of those three contractual years. When I looked him up in the 1970s, he took me to his special garage which was filled with beautiful works — works that were in every sense equal to anything the museums bought. But no museum was coming to buy any more Bruce Conner because he was no longer hooked up with the gallery system at the time.

Either Bruce broke the contract, or did not renew it; he was a sick man by the time it ended. He went back to his beloved San Francisco which, sadly, was much changed in the direction of New York by that time but was still sufficiently close to "Emerald City" that he could settle down and live there.

In a letter in 1979, Bruce wrote to me: "The legend [of his years with the gallery] is entertaining to me in retrospection since I have now dropped from the art world of exhibiting and won't read about contemporary art or go into museums or art galleries or teach. I have a different relationship now than I did in 1967 because I am not producing any art work at all."

After the contract, I think his low point was selling beads in a Hippie joint in Haight-Ashbury at $1.25 an hour, out of the absolute necessity to make some kind of living to feed his family. He was still suffering from ulcerative colitis to such an extent that he could not tolerate most foods; and it was very hard for him to go on a lecture tour, or go anywhere, because his diet had had to be so specialized.

I brooded a lot about Bruce. He stands as a sort of metaphor. I have devoted a great deal of my life trying to become at least famous enough to fight for the things I believe in — in the art world as well as in the whole society. Bruce actually went clear to the top, got his ulcers, got abused, mis-used, got some of his works purchased, and then collapsed out and, as far as the commercial world of sculpture was concerned, became completely forgotten, all within a few years.

All this had a considerable effect on Bruce. He had been from "the top," to selling beads in a Hippie joint, from health to serious, enduring illness. But he had been all the way through the system, you see. He was through and out the other side. He had his whole world of privacy intact, in a way that a person who has not achieved "the top" and given up his privacy cannot fully understand.

Still, Bruce has a wonderful sense of humor, which carried him through all those struggles. In those gallery-contract years, for instance, he once arrived at one of those required parties with his pockets loaded with buttons that said "I Am Bruce Conner." He breezed in and made his rounds, talking to people and pinning buttons on them until about fifty people were wearing "I Am Bruce Conner" buttons. Then he left. The gallery had to accept it, as it ended up making a good newspaper story. Bruce kept trying to rise above the adverse contingencies with his wit.

At another time, when he was serving on one of those seminars about Art, his wit let him get through again. The seminar consisted of about five grouchy men at a long table, all quarreling and growling at each other, and Bruce. The first day Bruce just sat there and said nothing. The next day, the moderator coaxed him to talk: "What do you think, Mr. Conner? What is your opinion, Mr. Conner?" He tried to "cool it" then with responses. But on the third day, he arrived inspired. He had noticed that all the others came in with brief cases, from which they pulled papers that they rummaged through during the seminar. So the third day Bruce, too, arrived with a brief case — a brief case full of marbles. When the others all opened their brief cases, Bruce opened his, and hundreds of marbles came bouncing out all over the floor and down into the audience. He spent the entire period picking up his marbles.

He was, too, a great one for making posters. He would make them for his friends, such as the one he did for Michael McClure. And at other times he would become very esoteric with them, making posters that advertised nothing at all — the poster itself was the event. These posters would appear to advertise something at first; they had all the aspects of an ordinary poster, but would say something like, "This Exists," and there would be pictures of, say, Jean Harlow and Billy the Kid without any reference to anything else.

One of Bruce's posters shows himself surrounded by five or six attractive women who are leaning on him, touching his hand and his suit. It is called "The Extraordinary Bruce Conner." His "Cosmic Ray" is the extraordinary Bruce Conner dealing with sex — and a lot more.

Again, one has to bear in mind that there are different versions of this film. The 16 mm one was made first. Then there are three 8 mm versions, numbered "1," "2" and "3." "Cosmic Ray #1" is a color print; that is, it has color inserts; and there are sepia-tone varieties of black and gray. It is made up of the last two thirds of the 16 mm version. "Cosmic Ray #2" has the remaining one-third of the 16 mm version repeated, plus new material that Conner edited to go with it; and it continues the movement. I think he speaks of "movement" in the sense of a musical movement. "Cosmic Ray #3" was completely new material. It is composed of new footage of the same woman who was in the 16 mm film, as well as other material.

All three of these versions were created to be shown together, to be run simultaneously; but they hold up beautifully as individual films. Conner says that "Cosmic Ray" is about censorship. But that is only one of the things it is about. "To talk about censorship," he says, "you have to show something of what is being censored. I regard censorship as death against life. Those forms that are used to kill people are those used for censorship. The organization which creates war, creates the army, is opposed to sex. They are opposed to procreation. . . . They [the Army] not only re-channel the creativity of men toward death by withdrawing them from the society of women, but they kill the fruit of the womb. This has something to do with the images in the film — the numbered leaders — the information which you were not supposed to see. The projectionist who controls the projector is not supposed to allow you to see that. That was very much more obviously true when these films were made. Censorship was much more obvious then. Now it has gone underground. We are presented with things that look like we are seeing everything when in fact we are not, which is much more pernicious than when we are simply told we are not permitted to look at certain things."

Sexploitation is what Conner concentrates on transforming in "Cosmic Ray." It is my suspicion that he is very much concerned with the exploitation of sex, just as his concern in "Report" is with the exploitation of President Kennedy's death. Similarly, he deals with sexploitation through TV and in the uses of advertising. He quotes these in ironic contexts, but there is something more to it than that. You get a perspective, as though you could look inside the mind that is affected by and imagining the multiplicity of sexual feedback.

The kinesiologist Ray Birdwhistle, who has studied body movement extensively, says that we are symmetrical along the backbone. As an example, there is now proof that for every muscle you use as you speak, there is a similar set of muscles in your anus that reflects the muscular movement of your lips — and vice versa. Maybe that is the reason people have problems with sexual expression in the history of art as it deals with sex. It has always been a problem in the arts to deal with sex as a subject and to produce a balanced, clear and thoughtful statement. Artists have found it difficult to observe sex and make a painting that is anything but either pornographic or an exaggeration of another sort, reflecting an inhibition of one kind or another. Conner's sex films stand among the very few art works that really do achieve a proportionate relationship between sex and their other subject matters.

As one watches "Cosmic Ray," one become aware that the evolution of Conner's different versions is away from sexual reference and more and more toward light — light as sensuosity, sexy light. Now, the original film's title is homage to jazz composer Ray Charles. The 16 mm film is set to the music of Ray Charles. But the

8 mm films, silent as they are, no longer pun upon the word "ray." They are singular in purpose; and the "ray" is singular with reference to light, at first the sensual shapes the light defines, then how it defines them. But the "ray" is intrinsically involved in the various rhythms of light defining these shapes – with a wide variety of contrasting rhythmic occurrences, flickering flares and extreme slow motion.

Light and certain shapes are very much concerns in Conner's work. Another of his 8 mm films, "Looking for Mushrooms," is an excellent example. Make no mistake, this is not simply a peyote documentary or a travelogue of Conner's Mexican sojourn; nor is it simply a "trip" movie. He titles his films accurately, so don't forget the word "looking" in the title. It is partly a word of instruction to the audience. We should be looking for mushrooms, mushroom shapes, references to mushrooms, peyote buttons, etc., throughout our experience of the film.

Some of these shapes and references occurred in the "Cosmic Ray" series – the umbrella of lights, the firework's mushrooms, the mushroom cloud, etc. In fact, Conner's obsession with this shape probably had as much to do with his making all these films as any involvement with the subject matter of each. Certain shapes and qualities of light proliferate and grow from film to film, spawning "children" (or kindred shapes) in each new work. Thus, the flowerings of "Looking for Mushrooms" become the essential subject of his "Easter Morning Raga"; and the rhythmic multiple body movements of the "Cosmic Ray" series become the stark flickering dance of singular consideration of his "Antonia," which is a sketch made in relation to the 16 mm film of Antonia dancing in "Breakaway."

"Antonia" and "Breakaway" both tend to seem as if Conner had literally torn the nude image free from the seduction implicit in both context and dance. The "cosmic rays" are, for instance, much more sexually arousing because of the quality of movement in each. "Breakaway" does, as the title advises, permit the freedom to experience sex as object – something many films advertise but do not deliver. It springs the trap of seductive image altogether. Pornography traps the viewer in seduction. Conner's films, even when seductive, comment on the process of seduction, so that it can be seen in operation.

It could be said that commentary is what Conner's films are all about. His film "Luke" is one short and sweet self-commentary upon the Hollywood movie "Cool Hand Luke," which starred Paul Newman. It is also, and thereby, a commentary on all Hollywood movies, and in that way, a commentary upon the whole illusion of "the movies," and finally, it is also in itself commenting upon Bruce Conner movies.

In this film, one can't help notice that the Hollywood workmen making "Cool Hand Luke" hardly seem to be working at all. They seem to drift about listlessly. Paul Newman, who is only acting as if he were working, seems to be performing all of Hercules' tasks at once; but then, as acting certainly is a job, he certainly is working even if the work is to act like he's working.

The comments a Conner film makes upon itself are always built of contradictions within contradictions – or perhaps we should say contravisions within contravisions. And in this film, "Luke," those large light reflectors which Hollywood uses to reflect back the sun permitted Conner to pun upon the contravision of the illusion of light itself.

My happiest story about Bruce Conner is one that says the most about the balance of his wit as we find it in his films. In watching his films, you find yourself feeling saddened, and then suddenly discover that you are laughing. His work is consistently filled with this quality, as in "Report" – this kind of contrary imagery, and more than that, imagery that elicits immediate contrary reactions in the psyche of practically everyone.

In the late 1960s I was scheduled, along with seven or eight other filmmakers, to go to Berlin. We were brought in on what you might call a "culture lift" over the Berlin Wall. In addition to lifting food in when "the Reds" blocked the overland supply routes, the U.S. government has rather regularly lifted culture into West Berlin. It does not work very well, actually.

We were all sent in to give them a shot at the American experimental film movement. We were put up at some god-awful culture house on the edge of town, and there I met Bruce Conner at the turn of the stairs, after not having seen him for several years. Without a moment's hesitation he came down and said, "How do you do? I am Stan Brakhage."

We went into East Berlin at one point, where we were continually subjected to harassment of a kind that can really be terrifying. This was nothing, of course, in comparison to what we would have felt if we'd truly been trapped there. But it was still far from enjoyable.

Conner's wit sustained me there a great deal. He had brought along Michael McClure's *Ghost Tantras*. This is a series of poems written close to the sonnet form but made up of beast language. A line from one of them, for example:

> Blue black wing space rainbow — Ghraaaaaar

These are very moving poems, if you read them aloud and put some feeling into them. McClure had asked his old buddy Bruce Conner to take the book and throw it over the Wall. So there we were, over the Wall in East Berlin, being followed, no less, after having been scared already by a number of little incidents. Bruce pulled out *Ghost Tantras* and threw it on a park bench. We walked about half a block, down what appeared to be an empty street, and then decided to walk back, as it was getting too dark. We turned around, back past the park bench, and the book was gone. This was the surest sign we had that we were being followed. But Bruce kept our spirits up by reminding us of what it must be like in the commissar's office as they went over *Ghost Tantras* looking for coded messages.

The other side of the Wall wasn't the best place, either, and finally we decided to leave a day early. It had become so oppressive there, that we just wanted to get out of Berlin altogether. Our nerves were stretched to the breaking point. So we went down to the airport to get the shuttle plane to Munich.

Now, I wanted to photograph our take-off, because the planes fly out over a huge graveyard in the center of town, and then directly over the Wall. I had told this to Bruce, that I wanted to get the graveyard and the Wall in 8 mm, to use in a film. At the airport, we went to the desk and asked if we could have a window seat — we would pay extra if it was necessary. The man at the desk said *"Nein"* — no window seats, absolutely impossible, in a stereotypical German way. We repeated that we were willing to pay, but the answer was still an emphatic *Nein*. He said that our only possibility would be to go and stand in line at the gate and, if we were the first in line, we might be able to get window seats. So we were given little red cardboard boarding passes, and, instead of catching breakfast, we went to sit on our luggage at the gate — the first in line.

By the time the plane came out on the field, an enormous line had formed behind us. An official took up his place at the door, ready to open the gate-chain. At that moment, a voice boomed over the loudspeaker, announcing in several languages that all those holding green passes will board the plane first. Bruce and I looked back down the line; all the passengers looked at their red passes, the same kind we held, then down at their shoes. Conner and I looked at each other in bafflement. What was this? A moment later, it was perfectly obvious what it was: here came a group of important-looking men and women, well-dressed and erect, all carrying green passes!

Conner began to argue with the official at the gate, and so did I. We explained that we had been there for two hours, that we'd been told it was just a matter of being first in line. We were creating quite a scene, and the German passengers were looking at us aghast.

Finally, Conner and I ducked under the chain and set out across the field, passing the well-to-do citizens with their green passes. We got fairly close to the plane before a military-police type of jeep came speeding to a halt right in front of us. Out jumped two big military police, stopping us with *"Nein, nein, nein,"* and again we started to argue while the men and women with the green slips walked past us.

At that point I realized that I did not particularly want to spend the night in a German jail, and was just about ready to give up, when Bruce broke out in a run. By then he was livid with beautiful American rage. He went right around the police and headed straight for the plane again. So I ran around the other side of the jeep, and then we were both running.

The police got into their jeep and came after us, and I was terrified. "This is it," I thought, "this is how it ends, being shot running across a German airfield trying to get a window seat." The jeep roared around in front of us, just as we got to the steps to the plane. They jumped out, and this time we could see that they really meant business.

They were saying, "You do not have red slips," and Conner was saying, "*Ja, ja,* we know," arguing back and forth, the police getting more and more stubborn and scary, until Conner said, "I *know*, I *know*! Heil Hitler!"

Well. Those two huge military policemen blanched. The whole line of passengers who were starting up the steps to the plane stopped. Brief cases dropped. Everything froze. With those two words, Bruce had named what had caused a world war.

But Bruce wasn't going to hang around and philosophize at that moment. While everyone stood there frozen, he ran around and climbed up the steps, outside the railing, into the plane and sat down in a window seat.

They never touched us again. They didn't serve us coffee or anything, but they didn't bother us again, either.

It's this story, I think, that says a lot about the strength of Bruce Conner. He exhibits the same kind of courageous stubbornness throughout his work — a tenacity of image — yet with American ease. It is the same sort of strength out of which he deals with everything in his films.

Photo: Mike Chikiris

Ken Jacobs

The particularities of Ken Jacobs' childhood read a little like a Charles Dickens' novel.

He was born in New York in 1933. Before he was born, his parents separated. He lived his first seven years with his mother, who was hospitalized much of the time, and with his maternal grandparents and an uncle and aunt in a house in Brooklyn. When he was seven years old, his mother died. He remembers those first seven years as a very warm time in his life – a happy, sheltered, warm feeling from his mother and a great feeling of affection and love between him and his grandmother. Ken says of his mother, "She was sick and hospitalized or out wage-earning most of the time. She was generous, playful, adoring, but also exotic to me – so often of necessity physically remote, I often couldn't get onto her whimsical and complex personality."

He remembers his grandparents as good grandparents, and he felt closely related to his Uncle Harry while he was living in that household. "He filled in adequately for my father," Ken says of his uncle. "I did lightly wonder, however, at the particularity of my situation in contrast to my friends in their two-parent homes. However, Uncle Harry could not provide what I demanded of him in later years. The night I visited him and he pointed to Eddie Fisher on television and said, 'Why can't you be like him?' freed me of the obligation to fake an appearance of family."

By the time his mother died, his father had remarried, and at the insistence of his father's new wife, Ken went to live with them, and really got acquainted with his father for the first time. He inherited a half-brother; and in spite of all the good intentions of these people, he was the Cinderella of the household. He was the bottom dog. As he recalls, during this period his father never referred to him as "Ken" or "Kenny," but always as "Stupid" or "Moron." And while he had been a happy child, his father so beat him down that he became a complete introvert, extremely nervous and subject to terrors and frights.

Then there was a second divorce, and he went with his father into a new marriage where he acquired a half-sister and another half-brother. In this third marriage, Ken's step-mother insisted that his father call him "Ken" or "Kenny," and he remembers this as part of the change. "My father made money during World War II," Ken says, "We had horses stabled next to Prospect Park in Brooklyn, and we moved to Hempstead, Long Island, to a big, gross house my father designed and built – twice, at a great money loss. The first structure, complete and furniture-filled, burned down two weeks before we were to move in – burnt explosively, really. My father was absolutely convinced it was anti-Semitic arson. Hate energized the rebuilding."

At fifteen Ken ran away from home and went to live with his grandmother and uncle and aunt. That did not work out. They were too old and/or felt it was an imposition. But he did have the opportunity to attend a better school, and he began to act on his interest in art. Having no one to play with, he had begun to read books at about the age of nine, which served to further separate him from other children.

As far as the rest of his childhood, Ken sums it up with: "Disastrous but typical, bequeathing me a social disgust and anger that I have cultivated, refined, monumentalized, and am gagging on."

For all his nervousness and sensitivity, Ken was forced to develop a very tough – or, as he calls it, "gutsy" – exterior in order to hold his own day to day.

There were some lucky breaks. As a pupil in the public school system, he had a pass to the Museum of Modern Art. One Saturday he went there and wandered down into the basement where they were showing films. He discovered that with his pass he could attend these films on certain days. So it was that at the age of fifteen or sixteen, Ken Jacobs saw most of the museum's collection of films, which included the French avant-garde works of Leger, Delluc, Man Ray, Rene Clair, Renoir, among others. These films thrilled him so much that at sixteen he began writing movie scripts, knowing that he was going to be a filmmaker.

In his high school years, music was also very important to Ken, not only to listen to, but as a sort of banner. He would play music so loudly that the neighbors complained. He was putting his tastes and sensibility up against his surroundings as noisily and dramatically as he could.

At sixteen, Ken was already a confirmed socialist — at least, he was on the extreme Left in all his attitudes. But even though he was becoming quite wise politically, as well as in other matters, he felt that he had to get a high school diploma; so he did finish high school. Still, the center of his considerations, the bright spot for him, were his excursions to the Museum of Modern Art, his books and his music.

By a curious coincidence, about this time Jonas Mekas and his brother Adolfas came over to the United States and began publishing their *Film Culture* magazine. They had a place in Brooklyn about two blocks from where Ken had lived with his grandparents. Ken did not meet the Mekases at that time, but he did go to a film showing that they put on in Manhattan, a showing of Eisenstein's "Alexander Nevsky." Later, of course, Jonas Mekas was to become very important in Ken's filmmaking life.

The Korean conflict was going full blast when Ken was in high school, and he was due to be drafted. By this time his attitudes were so strongly against anything this government was doing in international politics, and particularly the Korean War which Ken regarded as absolute imperialism, that he wrote a letter stating that he would not accept being drafted – that he had become a conscientious objector. However, he could not receive official conscientious objector status because he was not part of a recognized religious group that opposed fighting, and he could not bring himself to the hypocrisy of joining such a religion just to get the status. So in a final desperation, he enlisted in the Coast Guard which, as he had been told by a cousin, is essentially defensive and "does nothing." Even so, throughout his Coast Guard service, he felt miserable and guilty; he felt he was still aiding the cause of the "capitalist greed machine," as he put it. Ultimately, he applied for and got a transfer to the loneliest outpost the Coast Guard had, on an island off of Alaska, removed from everything.

In 1956, his stint in the Coast Guard was up, and he returned to New York, and almost immediately met a man who was going to be of tremendous importance in his development as an artist – Jerry Sims.

Now, Jerry Sims couldn't make a living. He was born to an old-world Brooklyn family. His father supported him even though he, too, was quite poor, because it would be the ultimate shame to the family if Jerry were to go on relief. Of course, the stipends from his father didn't amount to much; Sims was still picking up his cigarettes from the streets. But he had a brilliant mind and he was a tough, sharp, furious person. He lived in a small room with just four walls and a sink. The walls were covered with newspaper clippings. To Sims these pictures were all sharply related commentaries. He had made his entire room a kind of monumental scrapbook – or scrappy work of art – with clippings, photos, pin-ups and hang-ups of various kinds. Jerry Sims gave Ken Jacobs the beginnings of the understanding of how one can survive by creating an intense personal inner life. You might say that in a way this collection of Sims's stills was the first early powerful movie of Ken's life.

Another powerful influence on Ken at the time was one of the old-time journalist-photographers, Weegee. Weegee became very famous, partly because he was "in" with the Mafia. As Weegee put it, "When they were going to dump a body, they'd tell me where and when so I could get the picture." But it also happened that Weegee had a photographer's crazy magical sense always to get the impossible shots by seeming coincidence.

By the time Ken met Weegee he was retired from newspaper work. He had published a book which was of great importance to Ken, *The Naked City*, a book of his photographs. He had used the flashbulb in most of the photos in this book, going right up to people and flashing in their faces. The results were stark, flat photographs of dead white, intense, sickened, disturbed and falling-to-pieces faces.

Ken made much use of the technique in his films — the over-exposed face seen as nakedly as possible, so that many of the wrinkles that go to make up the mask of the face are bleached out, leaving a dead fish-belly face that looks stricken.

At this time Ken was going to City College of New York to study filmmaking. It was while he was in college that he began to realize the bedrock bottom of his existence — when there was nothing, he had nothing to lose, as he'd had nothing to lose in his Alaskan loneliness. Jerry Sims was almost an apostle of the philosophy: You had nothing, you were permitted to have nothing, there was no reason to think you ever would have anything, therefore you had absolutely nothing to lose.

At City College, Ken studied film, but he has said that he does not think he really learned anything there. However, from 1956 through 1959, he studied under Hans Hoffman, one of the greatest teachers of painting we have ever had in America. This intermittent studying under Hoffman reinforced something in Ken which otherwise, in his bitterness and terror and rock-bottomedness, might have been lost; that is, a deep exact appreciation of the arts and what the arts can do, of formalism and formalism within even a chaotic statement that the artist might be making.

In the beginning of his filmmaking Ken thought that there was some way he could make it in the commercial studios of the city, or that there would be something he could do that would pass as a documentary and perhaps get onto television. These ideas were vaguely in the back of his mind when, sometime before 1956, he had attempted to make a film on the Third Avenue Elevated. He failed at that, and he made several other attempts. Finally, he got together a little film called "Orchard Street."

He took "Orchard Street" to a friend who was a poet, and this friend had a musician friend, and they invited him to come over to their house to show it. When Ken arrived, he was surprised to see that the poet had invited some of the film art crowd to the showing, and he was terrified. Still, he showed the film, and all but a few attacked him, saying, "Oh, my god! How awful!" Most of them kept telling him what he *might* have done; they didn't see what he *had* done. Ken had tried to make a film that did not give one inch to any kind of slick polish and at the same time to give it a formality that was totally new. It was such an unaggressive, understated film, that the vociferous representatives of the film art crowd who were there rejected it entirely. Once again, it was a case of the "far-out" avant-garde group being the most bitchy, mean, conservative of all groups in the face of a new, alien "far out" artist. Ken, with his street-toughened exterior and his inner sensitivity, was not about to mix metaphors with these snobs, and left. (Years later, Ken learned that one of those few who remained silent that evening was Jonas Mekas, who had come there to read his Lithuanian poetry.)

Ken Jacobs never came to terms with the "art crowd" of New York. He rejected it totally.

So he abandoned the delusions of making it commercially or fitting in with the current elite of film art. Then came years during which he suffered terrible poverty. He was eating fish that were thrown away at the Fulton Fish Market. He was living off of women — he would find a girlfriend and she would feed him. The situation was desperate. At one point he got a job as a janitor, but even then he was paid so little that he still had to walk from his place on 57th Street to the Fulton Fish Market and back for want of subway fare.

Surviving in New York wasn't very easy, especially for an artist who was as intent on his vision as Ken. New York was not the "Emerald City," or anything like it. There were many reasons why it wasn't. One was that, culturally, it was tied to Europe, so that European artists – at that time, the surrealists, especially – found an immediate home there. In fact, anyone coming into the New York art milieu with a European accent could more easily "make it" than someone who had come in with a southern drawl or a Kansas twang.

One would roam around the city trying to find a room with some standards of cleanliness, but when you had counted the money in your pocket, you would end up in a one- or two-room wreck on the lower east side with walls so thin that every time someone bumped against them, new cracks appeared. The walls in these "artists' apartments" of the time were actually so thin that you could listen to your neighbors, not only fighting or fucking, but whispering. If you were lucky enough to have a bathtub, it would be tiny, and in the kitchen with a board over it so it could double as your kitchen table. The water would trickle from the tap so slowly that, even if it had been hot, it would be cold by the time the tub was full. Cold and rusty. The filth was unbelievable. "Jungle" is not the term to describe it because there is no jungle so dirty as a lower east side apartment in the 1950s. In the apartment that I lived in, for example, if you walked into the kitchen late at night and turned on the light, literally thousands of black spots would scurry to the walls. The cockroach became the ultimate symbol of the whole scene, the wildlife of this jungle. Now, I normally don't go out of my way to kill insects, but I can remember struggling to beat those things into some kind of submission.

So there were the artists, living in a milieu where first they were suspect for living there at all by those in authority – the local police – and on the other hand, unaccepted by the neighborhood of minority groups who were holding together fiercely and tenaciously and defending their positions in order to maintain the few vestiges of dignity left to them in those slums.

These were the grubby daily terms of survival in New York at that time. Here was a city with the greatest theaters, but you couldn't afford to see a play or a concert. But some did manage to. There was, for instance, a young artist, Carolee Schneemann, with whom I loved to go out. She would pick up things at Goodwill or other thrift stores, like an outrageously moth-eaten boa, and she had the chutzpah to appear at Carnegie Hall, saying she was the Countess So-and-so in such a manner that they would let her in for fear she would otherwise create a scene. She would say, "Tickets for Countess von Schneemann and party," and puff herself up regally. Often, I would be standing there trembling, expecting to be arrested at any moment, but finally they would come up with the tickets, and we would get our seats in the second or third row and listen to the concert.

In the 1950s, film as an art form in New York was centered around several people. Maya Deren had come there from Los Angeles with Sasha Hammid, and almost single-handedly began showing her films and the ones she and Sasha had made together. She was the first to really open up shop and begin arranging her own film shows — and succeeding with them. Maya Deren is still referred to as "the mother of us all." Ken says that he always called Maya about twice a year to ask her for money. She had a foundation that was much written about, but actually never had enough money to give any awards or grants. Ken would call her and she would say, "Call me in the fall." He would call her again in the fall, and she would say, "Give me a call in the spring." For a while he thought she was just putting him off. But the fact is that no one ever gave Maya Deren any significant amount of money to give to any filmmakers, and the foundation was mostly myth.

There were other people making films, too, some too shy to show their work publicly, who had to be persuaded to have little showings. One of these was Ian Hugo, who had married Anais Nin. Ian and Anais had all the senses of what it meant to be an artist, as is clear in her writings.

There was also Jack Smith, whose films include "Flaming Creatures." In 1956 Ken met Jack through Bob Fleischner, a fellow CCNY student. At first, Ken thought that Jack's work was, in his words, "too patterned after Mad Comics, derivative and forced." He didn't think much of Jack himself at their first meeting, either: "Shrill. Tedious to me. His friends were lost, self-image-conscious children." But his feeling about Jack and Jack's work soon changed. "In a month or two," he says, "I began to catch on to his original qualities."

Jack Smith was a little bit older than Ken. He came from Ohio, as did a younger man, Hollis Frampton whom Ken would meet much later. Of Jack Smith's influence, Jacobs says, "Some very basic decisions would be made, values set, during my collaboration with Smith, including some involvements Jack then disapproved of but came around to later . . . my 'junk' collecting and junk-object, junk-scape structuring." Primarily, Jack encouraged Ken to stay alive, which is the most important influence of all. He, and later, Hollis, were people who recognized Ken's work and understood him, and with whom he could feel companionship.

Jack was an actor and had had aspirations toward Hollywood, but by then he had recognized that he did not care to make it as an actor, and he began making his own movies, parodies of Hollywood. They were done out of a deep appreciation for that world which he knew he would never be a part of. By the time Ken met him, Jack had been working on a film for about four years called "Buzzards of Baghdad."

But Jack did become a "star" in Ken's films. He's in "Blonde Cobra," opposite Jerry Sims, and in several others, including "Little Stabs at Happiness" and "The Death of PTown." In "Saturday Afternoon Blood Sacrifice," it is Smith, dressed up as the Pope, who does the wild dance in the streets of New York. As it happened, during the shooting, a policeman was drawn to this event and questioned Ken, who went right on filming the confrontation. The complete form of this film was not presented until 1964.

That is a quality of all of Ken's work – the length of time he takes to complete a film while he weaves varieties of years into his considerations of it. In fact, Ken felt it excruciating even to contemplate the finishing of a work. It is almost as if he does not regard anything as finished. He also uses material from one film in others; material flies back and forth in all his films. For instance, footage was taken from "Orchard Street" and from "Little Cobra Dance" and put into "Star Spangled to Death," a work which he began in 1958, and which also stars Jack Smith. It wasn't until 1972 that Ken started putting "Star Spangled to Death" into its final form.

From 1958 to 1960, then, Ken was working very consciously on "Star Spangled to Death" as well as beginning the shooting on what was to become "Little Stabs at Happiness." And he was having showings to raise money. When he had the first showing of "Star Spangled to Death" as a work-in-progress, the audience was outraged at its length. Later, in desperation, he committed what I regard as a very black act for an artist. He knew what it was that had bothered the audience, so he cut all that out and presented a shorter version composed of the parts that he thought they might like. But even after this cutting, very few liked the film and again it was unprofitable. So in 1972 he began the work of putting the film back into its original long form.

Ken posed the question better than anyone else, and he posed it right off the top of the deck: "What is art? It is not craft." That is such an obvious statement of the fact that we cannot regard art, or judge it, as related to its craft. But Ken was the first one in film to state the basic premise. His intention was to defeat every instance where craft might seduce an audience. I do not say that he always succeeded. In fact, I think some of the most beautiful moments in his films – and I mean beautiful as an art – occur when there is some seduction, some craftiness even. But the most unique moments are when his craft is utterly defeated, when the film is so abrasive you can hardly stand it, but it is clearly formal as hell. "Hell" is a good word here, as it was the condition of the time for him.

When he had finished his first version of "Little Stabs at Happiness," he took it to the Charles Theater to show. In those days, if you brought a film to the Charles on Saturday night, you were admitted free, and your film would be shown along with those of other filmmakers. So Ken took "Little Stabs at Happiness" there, but he was worried about what sort of reaction it would bring. Much to his surprise, half the audience liked it and were enthusiastic. The other half disliked it with equal enthusiasm, which resulted in one of those booing-and-applauding matches throughout the entire showing. This sort of thing is funny to remember, but at the time it was terrifying. Many artists refuse to have any shows at all for fear of having to go through something like Ken went through that Saturday evening.

In 1960, Bob Fleischner gave Ken the footage from which "Blonde Cobra" was made. The year before, Bob had been making a film with Jack Smith. A fire broke out in his kitchen, and much of the raw footage was destroyed, along with footage from another film. The two films were to have been "Blonde Venus" and "The Cobra Woman." Fleischner gave the surviving footage from both of these films to Ken, and from these rolls, Ken edited his own film, "Blonde Cobra," and evolved a soundtrack integral to the film. It is a remarkable soundtrack, composed of Jack Smith's artful, hysterical sounding monologues. When Ken was putting "Blonde Cobra" together, there was no thought that any audience anywhere would ever look at it. The material, which otherwise Fleischner would have thrown away, had an intense personal meaning to Ken: it represented a life that flaunted itself desperately and bravely, insisting on self-completedness however bizarre the circumstances.

The following year, 1961, Ken and Jack went to Provincetown out of that kind of desperation many of us indulged in — a desperation that was heavily salted with a sense of lively, good-humored adventure. By this time they had gone through a period of not speaking to each other, but now they were friendly again, and collaborating on a number of things, including short stories and performances. With very little in their pockets, they staged a revue in the cocktail lounge of the Seahorse Inn in Provincetown — a three-person show with Martha the Scorch, titled "The Human Wreckage Revue." It was shut down after several performances, alas.

They had brought some film with them, and it was in Provincetown that Ken shot footage for what was to become "The Death of PTown." Down on the beach, Ken shot Jack as a screaming vampire flitting across the sands. This creature was, as Ken puts it, "aesthetically wounded by the commercially uglified Provincetown/America."

Shortly later, Jack began working on his film "Flaming Creatures." By this time, he had resumed his own life in filmmaking. Unfortunately, he and Ken became estranged. I think the essential reason was that, while they were in Provincetown, Ken had met Flo. Their relationship was probably intolerable to Jack at that point, because Jack had "come out of the closet" and was realizing his gayness. I think that one of the saddest moments in Ken's life was the final break with Smith. Their parting was extremely bitter, and that bitterness held on for years.

By 1962, Ken had met Jonas Mekas. Mekas' influence on film — and in Ken's life — was overwhelming. Jonas offered to raise the money to print Ken's "Blonde Cobra" and "Little Stabs at Happiness." At last Ken would have the first prints of these works.

As it happened, when Ken first showed "Blonde Cobra" at the Film Makers' Co-op, I had just arrived from Colorado, and I was feeling very out of sorts with the whole film movement, convinced that it was being taken over by druggies and pseudo-revolutionaries.

When I saw on the screen what looked like total dishevelment, expressions of the very anarchistic attitudes that I was feeling had overtaken filmmaking at the time, I began to mouth off about the film. That, alas, was the first meeting between Ken and me. Within a few years, however, I came to recognize "Blonde Cobra" as one of the masterpieces in the American cinema.

By 1963 Ken was really getting in contact with other artists in New York. It was the year that he met the filmmakers Willard Maas and Marie Menken. Willard had also gained fame as a poet, particularly in the 1930s, and Marie also had some renown as a painter and collagiste. They lived in Brooklyn Heights, in a rent-controlled penthouse which they had managed to secure during the Depression and hold onto. It looked for all the world like a ship that had been wrecked on top of an apartment house. Ken visited Willard and Marie in their penthouse, and was chewed out by Willard for not having a beginning, middle and end to his films.

Willard's criticisms didn't upset Ken as they might have earlier in his life; he had begun to feel that there was a general comprehension of his work. He saw that new forms were arising from many people who also had had bitterly insufficient childhoods. The roots of it can be seen clearly in his 1964 film, "Window." There is nothing to this film whatever if one does not understand what it is to be stuck with your window that looks out on the meanest, cruelest scene — the shabbiest of walls. Your window looks out on the scrubbiest brick and god-damnedest dirty surroundings conceivable. It represents the whole emotional suffering of your life. Your parents are that window to the world, your school is that wall, and your spirit has had to live through it. Here is a man up against that window and those walls, making his entire articulation out of this desperation. "Window" could be thrown out of focus and its very rhythms alone would articulate a meaning. People saw that meaning, that feeling, in "Window," and many appreciated it.

By 1964, a change began to occur for Ken which was profound and at the same time normal within the culture of artists. Having survived and having received some recognition, from even a few people, one begins to realize that one has created something. The filmmaker looks at his works and shows them to some friends or perhaps even a large audience, and begins to see that they hold up, that they have a form of integrity. And this all happens much to the artist's surprise. Ken Jacobs, by 1964, began to be accepted.

Now, mind you, he wasn't accepted by society at large. In fact, in 1964 at the Bridge Theater, at a showing of Jack Smith's "Flaming Creatures," he was arrested and spent some time in jail. Ken was managing the Bridge (Filmmaker's Showcase) and Flo was selling tickets. The showing was raided by the police, and Ken and Flo, along with Jonas Mekas, were arrested. Ken was always caught in that kind of trap. Every job he stumbled into, every opportunity, seemed to backfire on him. But he had begun to have a home with Flo; it was his retreat. And he and Flo were expecting a baby.

When one is young, in his or her twenties, one can deal with the world by sparring with it, always on one's toes; but at some point a person is either going to drop dead from that intensity or is going to begin to learn to stand still and have a look at things. Ken began to recognize that he couldn't continue on that nervous, frenzied level. His life started to undergo a total change of pace, to quiet down.

There is a way to express this "stillness" in film, by not touching the camera at all. Most widely known for this technique, of course, is Andy Warhol, who set up his camera and turned it on and walked away from it. It's difficult to imagine anyone who hasn't read about or heard of Warhol's arranged "magic occasions," where people would wander in and out of the film's image — set-ups for the camera simply to operate as a machine. Ken Jacobs' form of this recognition of the camera as a machine is one that I value as having much more integrity that Warhol's. Warhol's work seems to me to fall within an anthropological genre; whereas Ken's has the psychological balances and proportions that shape an art as distinct from a record.

In the middle 1960s Ken began expressing himself as well through a series of shadow plays and became involved in the "happenings" of that period. He staged some "happenings" with Ken Dewey and worked with Terry Riley, and he also staged some of his own. It was a series of pieces which he thought of as chapters in "an evolving novel of despair, with the compensation of exquisite articulation and victory in aesthetic accomplishment." The first one was called "The Big Blackout of '65," which refers to the city-wide electrical outage of that year. Chapter 1 of "The Big Blackout of '65" was titled "The Thirties Man"; Chapter 2 was "Slide of the City"; Chapter 3 was "Give Me the Moon Anytime"; and Chapter 4 was "Evoking the Mystery." These were presented at a church in Greenwich Village. The audience would arrive and sit down. Occasionally, an organ would sound a note, shadowy figures would move across the walls, creaky doors would open and shut. People would move about with lights. Most of the performance was done with lights and shadows and Ken playing the organ. His organ-playing, I would say, was inspired by the music of Olivier Messian, another of the artists whose friendship I share with Ken, as we share the friendships of Jonas Mekas and the great artist and filmmaker, Joseph Cornell, and many others.

Around this same time, Ken's circle was growing to include Michael Snow and Hollis Frampton. Michael Snow had come to New York and moved to lower Manhattan with his wife Joyce Weiland. He came to New York almost as though escaping from his Canadian fame as a painter, and he began to revive his earlier interest in film as an art form. Perchance, he lived within a few blocks of Ken and Flo. In 1966 Hollis Frampton gravitated to the city. He, too, had worked his way through a number of forms in the arts and was beginning to be interested in the possibilities of film as art.

(Coincidentally, Frampton — as well as, in time, filmmakers Ernie Gehrard and Andrew Norin — was from a little town in Ohio not far from Jack Smith's home town.)

So Michael Snow and Joyce Weiland, Ken and Flo Jacobs, and Hollis Frampton became friends and, fairly regularly, got together with one another "around the kitchen table." They talked film, they showed their films to each other and ideas, possibilities, were hatched. It's a common enough phenomenon among artists who feel the sort of affinity for each other that these people felt. You end up with a kind of field of possibilities as an art eventually, but no one is thinking about it as an art when it's going on — just as a field of possibilities. Individuals are tangential to this field; they gaze at each other across it, and each works from his or her own corner of it. The particular field here can be traced very easily, as well as what brings Ken Jacob to it. It is a reaction against continuing to make it with only one's raw nerves; and it brought him to making "Soft Rain," his 1968 film in which his window returns.

In "Soft Rain" Ken has pasted onto that window a piece of black paper, and this makes a lot of compositional "wit's end" because of the artificial canyon which the paper created. It was important to Ken, however, that the paper be seen as paper at the same time as its effect be seen; and for that reason he moves it slightly in the beginning.

"Soft Rain" contains a wealth of subtle wit. It is, for example, composed of one roll of film which is repeated. I am always delighted when an audience recognizes this. I had seen the film seven or eight times before I did, and even when I recognized it, I could so little believe it that I asked Ken, very hesitatingly, "Ken, is it really so, or am I mistaken? Is that the same roll repeated?" He said, "Yes, of course!" This is an extremely witty and humorous statement about the limitations of seeing and the fact that a scene is inexhaustible. Many people, seeing this film, do not recognize the same figures moving across the screen, and so it is a continually new drama to them, even though it literally is repetition. Once one is delighted by seeing "Soft Rain," how can one ever be bored again? Even "Window" challenges boredom by showing that though life does repeat, there is no excuse for boredom.

In the late 1960s, before he made "Soft Rain," Ken went through an awesome experience, but one that brought him recognition. He was appointed to create a workshop for filmmakers on the lower east side, as part of a government project. He named it "The Millenium Film Workshop," and in the hands of such an artist as Ken Jacobs it was shaped into a functional existence of which the present Millenium Workshop is a third- or fourth-generation descendant. It was a beautiful and powerful institution, but there were those within it who were opposed to Ken's policies and methods and waged a major battle against him until he was kicked out. Most of the students went with Ken, and he began lending them equipment and helping them on a private basis. But at least for this brief period he held a steady position and received a government salary to create and maintain a workshop for young filmmakers.

After "Soft Rain," a very important thing happened in Ken's life. He was hired to teach, first at St. John's College in Queens, then at Binghampton, State University of New York, and to create a film department with Larry Gottheim. They started from scratch, supported by state funds (which have since been reduced), and got the film department going, purchasing films and enabling students to get degrees in filmmaking. Ken's life was changed enormously.

In that terror of new position, Ken began working directly out of himself to confront the unnervy camera — the unheld camera — to confront directly the facts of his life. The result can be seen in his film called "Nissan Ariana Window," which is the full name of his and Flo's daughter, Nissan Ariana Window Jacobs."

This film begins with the hard "pop" images, then shows Flo, pregnant and increasingly aware of the camera. That is something to watch for in Ken Jacobs' films. There is an increasing awareness of the camera on the part of the "actors," which anyone else might cut out and throw away.

Flo is sitting there with milk dripping from her breasts. Then the tension increases from this hard flat image of a bucolic, beautifully naked woman. A cat is introduced. The cat rubs against Flo's leg — this just happens, but Ken weaves it through the plot, much as a composer would weave an oboe sound through a symphony. There is a lessening of tension as Flo strokes the cat. Then we move quickly to other scenes, like the kitchen sink (this film has everything in it, including the kitchen sink); the wash on the line — a hard-edged image; the romantic image of ducks on a lake, the kind of euphoria a young husband feels as he waits for the baby to be born. Then there is the baby, Nisi, in her crib, being cared for. Ken makes much use of the crib — the fact of the baby's crib having bars. The first thing the child sees is through bars, as in a jail. Then there is the scene of Nisi on the rug, and this is the archetypal triumph of the film — the father photographing his baby on the rug. The most normal thing becomes, in this film, the most surrealistic image that Ken Jacobs has ever produced.

Ken had always been fascinated by all aspects of film; some of them that interested him most were "B" movies. He used to love to go to 42nd Street and see them. He would get the most excited over those moments when the actors would slam a door and the whole set would shake because it was made of cloth, or the moments when an actor would forget his or her lines and the camera just kept on going because it was a low-budget movie. Those were the moments when the craft of seductive movie-making was stripped bare.

Ken turned to film history's beginning when he took a film called "Tom, Tom, the Piper's Son," which is an interesting film but certainly not a work of art. It was photographed by Billy Bitzer, Griffith's cameraman, before, I believe, Bitzer knew Griffith. It is a primitive, or naive, early crank-'em-out American movie, but it is unusually concerned with detail; something of an experiment in its day. In those days, moviemakers grabbed any plot line they could think of and made the movie up as they went along. So you have Tom Tom the piper's son at a fair, where Tom Tom steals a pig and runs away, and the people chase him here, there, everywhere. Ken fell in love with this movie. He began working with it, rephotographing images from the screen. The result is hilarious.

Ken's "remake" begins with the movie as it was made; then he begins moving his camera in on the scene, making his own frames of the scenes, picking out one figure, then another, slowing the projector and rephotographing again and again, much as if up against that window, and in the process, his film expands to make a metaphor of all human endeavor. Throughout, there is sexual symbolism and metaphor. Tom Tom climbs up the chimney and jumps out of it, then all the people who are pursuing him do the same. It is a long orgiastic scene, as well as being much else Bitzer never thought about. This scene seems long even in Bitzer's version, but Ken has extended it to its ultimate, so that this chimney becomes a gateway to a world of infinite possibilities, and it is hysterically funny. Jokes emerge that were never intended in the original, and the jokes that were in the original are expanded to entirely different levels of humor. Ken's "Tom Tom" is probably an ultimate comedy. It takes a simple comedy that was cranked out in the dawn of the film industry and reaches all the way to the fullest possibilities of comedy that I have ever seen in one film.

In rearing his daughter, Nisi, Ken wanted to allow her complete freedom, to shower affection and love on her, and not restrict her, as much of his childhood had been a hell of restriction. It was not just a case of spoiling the child — nothing as stupid as that — but was more a philosophy along the lines of Summerhill's S. Neal, giving the child every break possible within reason. As a result, Nisi is a very beautiful child, warm, open and sensitive. Sometimes, however, her sensitivity can be an agony.

There is a story which Hollis Frampton tells that points up Nisi's ultra sensitivity. Ken does not approve of much that is shown on television, so he buys old Castle films from the 1930s, animated films and early film drama, to show Nisi. One time, as Hollis tells it, Ken brought one home for her before he had had the opportunity to preview it — he had seen only the first five minutes, enough to see that it was the animated story of a little girl who, with her nanny, takes her doll out to the park. Great for Nisi, he thought, and so he set up the projector to watch the movie. After the first five minutes, though, things start to take a bad turn. The little girl's doll gets lost, and it starts to rain, and the nanny has to get the little girl home. She is crying and calling for her doll and being dragged off; and there is a heartbreaking scene of the doll lying in the grass and the rain pouring down and ruining its painted face. Nisi, who had already begun to be upset, was by now weeping.

But Ken felt sure that all would come out happily in the end — after all, the first five minutes had been so sweet and sentimental. But things go from worse to worst: the lost doll is attacked by dogs in the park, then crawls around looking for the little girl. By the time the doll reaches the little girl's house, both Nisi and Flo were sobbing. But Ken kept the movie running, thinking, yes, the happy ending must be coming up when they saw the doll climbing up the drainpipe to the little girl's window. But no! The doll looks into the window and sees the little girl with a new, clean, pretty doll with eyes that open and close. The bedraggled doll looks at herself in the glass and realizes she is finished, and crawls back down the drainpipe and throws herself in the gutter.

At this point, Ken was still hoping against hope that the little girl would see her old doll the next morning and rescue it. But in the final scene, the little girl comes out of the house in the morning with her new doll and walks right past the old one in the gutter, and goes laughing happily down the street. Nisi, of course, was in a state of shock.

Ken would rather show happy-ending films to his daughter, but he works against happy endings in his own films. He works to achieve a balance proportionate to his experience of life. Essentially, Ken is confronted newly now, not as someone desperately trying to survive and being shut out in every instance, but as a recognized filmmaker and a teacher. As a teacher he is highly respected; and his films are being written about. He is being recognized. He is an established American artist in the twentieth century.

•

Filmographies

Compiled and edited by Robert Haller

James Broughton (1913 -)

The Potted Psalm (1948, with Sidney Peterson): b/w, 25 minutes
Mother's Day (1948): b/w, 22 minutes
Adventures of Jimmy (1950): b/w, 11 minutes
Loony Tom (1951): b/w, 10½ minutes
Four in the Afternoon (1951): b/w, 15 minutes
The Pleasure Garden (1953): b/w, 38 minutes
The Bed (1968): color, 20 minutes
Nuptiae (1969): color, 14 minutes
The Golden Positions (1970): b/w toned, 32 minutes
This Is It (1971): color, 10 minutes
Dreamwood (1972): color, 45 minutes
High Kukus (1973): color, 3 minutes
Testament (1974): color, 20 minutes
The Water Circle (1975): color, 3 minutes
Erogeny (1976): color, 6 minutes
Together (1976, with Joel Singer): color, 8 minutes
Windowmobile (1977, with Joel Singer): color, 8 minutes
Song of the Godbody (1977, with Joel Singer): color, 11 minutes
Hermes Bird (1979): color, 11 minutes
The Gardener of Eden (1981, with Joel Singer): color, 8½ minutes
Shaman Psalm (1981, with Joel Singer): color, 7 minutes
Devotions (1983, with Joel Singer): color, 22 minutes

Scattered Remains (1988, with Joel Singer): color, 14 minutes
Film Rental Sources: Canyon Cinema, San Francisco; Film-Makers' Cooperative, New York
Documentation: Anthology Film Archives; Kent State University Libraries

Bruce Conner (1933 -)

A Movie (1958): b/w, 12 minutes
Cosmic Ray (1962): b/w, 4 minutes
Leader (1964): b/w, 35 minutes (No longer extant.)
Vivian (1965): b/w, 3 minutes
Ten Second Film (1965): b/w, 10 seconds (The entire film was reproduced as a poster by the New York Film Festival.)
Breakaway (1966): b/w, 5 minutes
Looking for Mushrooms (1967): color, 3 minutes
Report (1967): b/w, 13 minutes
The White Rose (1967): b/w, 7 minutes
Liberty Crown (1967): b/w, 5 minutes (No longer extant.)
Permian Strata (1969): b/w, 3½ minutes
Marilyn Times Five (1973): b/w, 13½ minutes
Crossroads (1976): b/w, 36 minutes
Take the 5:10 to Dreamland (1976): b/w, 5 minutes, 10 seconds
Valse Triste (1977): b/w with sepia tone tint, 5 minutes
Mongoloid (1978): b/w, 3½ minutes
America is Waiting (1981): b/w, 3½ minutes

8 mm Films

Cosmic Ray I, II, III (1965): b/w, color, 3½ minutes each
Looking for Mushrooms (1965): color, 11 minutes (at 5 frames per second)
Class Picture (1965): b/w, 3½ minutes
Easter Morning Raga (1966): color, 11 minutes (at 5 frames per second)
Luke (1966): color, 11 minutes (at 5 frames per second)
Report (1964-68): b/w, 3½ minutes
Coming Attractions (1968): b/w, 3 minutes
Antonia (late 1960s): b/w, approx. 10 minutes

Film Rental Sources: Museum of Modern Art, New York; One Way Films, San Francisco (rentals and videocassette sales)
Documentation: Anthology Film Archives

Maya Deren (1917 - 1961)

Meshes of the Afternoon (1943, with Alexander Hammid): b/w. 13¾ minutes
Witch's Cradle (1943): unfinished
At Land (1944): b/w, 15 minutes
The Private Life of a Cat (1945, with Alexander Hammid): b/w, 30 minutes
[There is considerable dispute whether Deren's part in making this film went beyond its conception: the author's assumption that Maya Deren was a photographer in this film derives from first hand conversation with her, circa 1955. — RH]
A Study in Choreography for Camera (1945): b/w, 2½ minutes [Deren credited choreographer Talley Beatty, who is onscreen during the entire film, as co-director, although he had no part in the editing — RH]
Ritual in Transfigured Time (1946): b/w, 14½ minutes
Meditation on Violence (1948): b/w, 13 minutes
Medusa (1949): unfinished
Ensemble for Somnabulists (1951): unfinished
Haitian film footage (1947 - 51): unfinished (The footage was finally edited after Deren's death by Teiji and Cherel Ito and released as *Divine Horsemen: The Living Gods of Haiti*. b/w, 52 minutes.)
The Very Eye of Night (1952-55; released 1959): b/w, 15 minutes
Haiku film project (1959-60): unfinished

Film Rental Sources: Museum of Modern Art, New York; Film-Makers' Cooperative, New York
Videocassette Sales: Mystic Fire Video, New York; McPherson & Company, Publishers
Documentation: Anthology Film Archives

Jerome Hill (1905 - 1972)

Tom Jones (1927, with Bill Hinkle): b/w, 150 minutes
The Magic Umbrella (1927): completed but not released until 1971 as part of *Film Portrait*
The Fortune Teller (1932): completed but not released until 1971 as part of *Film Portrait*
Snow Flight (1938): not in distribution (Released by Warner Brothers as *Ski Flight.)*
Seeing Eye (1940): not in distribution
Grandma Moses (1950): not in distribution
Salzburg Seminar (1950): not in distribution
Cassis, or *How to Be Happy though Healthy* (1950): not in distribution
Albert Schweitzer (1957): color, 81 minutes
The Sand Castle (1961): b/w and color, 65 minutes
Open the Door and See All the People (1964): b/w, 82 minutes
Schweitzer and Bach (1965): color, 13½ minutes
Anti-Corrida, or *Death in the Forenoon,* or *Who's Afraid of Ernest Hemingway* (1933; released 1965): color, 2 minutes
The Artist's Friend (1966): color, 4½ minutes
Merry Christmas (1969): completed but not released until 1971 as part of *Film Portrait*
Canaries (1968): color, 4 minutes
Film Portrait (1971): color, 80½ minutes

Film Rental Source: Film-Makers' Cooperative, New York (films from 1957)
Documentation: Anthology Film Archives

Ken Jacobs (1933 -)

Orchard Street (1956): unfinished
Saturday Afternoon Blood Sacrifice: TV Plug: Little Cobra Dance (1957/ 1964, with Jack Smith): b/w, 9 minutes
Star Spangled to Death (1957): b/w and color, shown in various editings and varying lengths of time between two and four hours
Little Stabs at Happiness (1958/ 1963): color, 15 minutes

Blonde Cobra (1959/1963): b/w and color, 33 minutes
The Death of PTown (1961): color, 7 minutes
Baudlarian Capers (1963-74): unfinished; b/w and color, 20 minutes
We Stole Away (1964): color, approx. 90 minutes (unfinished)
Window (1964): color, 12 minutes
Lisa and Joey in Connecticut, January '65: "You've Come Back" "You're Still Here!" (1965): color, 28 minutes, sound on tape
Naomi Is A Vision of Loveliness (1965, 8 mm): color, 4 minutes
Nissan Ariana Window (1966): color, 21 minutes
Airshaft (1967): color, 4 minutes
Soft Rain (1968): color, 12 minutes
Tom Tom the Piper's Son (1969, revised 1971): b/w and color, 115 minutes
Nissan Ariana Window (1969): color, 14 minutes
Globe (formerly *Excerpt From the Russian Revolution*) (1969): color, 3-D, 22 minutes
Urban Peasants (1974): b/w and color, 60 minutes
The Doctor's Dream (1978): b/w, 23 minutes
The Winter Footage (1964-65/1984): color, 42½ minutes
The Perfect Film (1986): b/w, 21¾ minutes
Jerry Takes a Back Seat, Then Passes Out of the Picture (1987 [shot 1975]): color, 13 minutes
The Sky Socialist (1964-65/1988): color, 90 minutes

Cine-Theater Works (a selection), involving shadowplay or film: *The Big Blackout of '65: Chapter One "Thirties Man"* (1965); *Restful Moments* 2- and (1st) 3-dimensional show (1970); *A Good Night for the Movies (II): 4th of July by Charles Ives by Ken Jacobs* (1972); *A Man's Home is His Castle Films: The European Theater of Operations* (1974); *" 'Slow is Beauty' -Rodin"* 2- and 3-dimensional shadowplay (1975); *The Boxer Rebellion* 2- and 3-dimensional shadowplay (1975); *Flop: 4th of July, 1976; Ken Jacobs at the Console performing "Stick to Your Carpentry and You Won't Get Nailed"* (1979).

Nervous System performances (two-projector works deriving 3-D from standard 2-D archival film): *The Impossible* [chapters one through five, 1975-1980]; *XCXHXEXRXRXIXEXSX* (1980); *Ken Jacob's Theater of Unconscionable Stupidity Presents Camera Thrills of the War* (1981); *The Whole Shebang* (1982); *Making Light of History: "The Philippines Adventure"* (1983).

Film Rental Source: Film-Maker's Cooperative, New York
Documentation: Anthology Film Archives

Christopher MacLaine (1923 - 1975)

The End (1953): color, 34¾ minutes
The Man Who Invented Gold (1957): color, 14 minutes
Beat (1958): color, 6 minutes
Scotch Hop (1959): color, 5½ minutes
[MacLaine may also be the maker of *Moods in Motion*, a film apparently made in 1954 — RH]

Film Rental Source: Film-Maker's Cooperative

Marie Menken (1910 - 1970)

Visual Variations on Noguchi (1945): b/w, 7 minutes
Hurry! Hurry! (1957): color, 4 minutes
Glimpse of the Garden (1957): color, 4 minutes
Dwightiana (1957): color, 3½ minutes
Faucets (1960): unfinished
Eye Music in Red Major (1961): color, 5½ minutes
Arabesque for Kenneth Anger (1961): color, 6 minutes
Bagatelle for Willard Maas (1961): color, 5½ minutes
Moonplay (1962): color, 5 minutes
Mood Mondrian (1963): color, 7 minutes
Drips and Strips (1963): color, 2½ minutes
Notebook (1963): color, 10 minutes
Go Go Go (1963): color, 12 minutes
Drips in Strips (1963): color, 2½ minutes
Wrestling (1964): b/w, 8 minutes
Andy Warhol (1965): color, 22 minutes
Lights (1966): color, 6½ minutes
Sidewalks (1966): b/w, 6½ minutes
Watts With Eggs (1967): color, 2½ minutes

Excursion (1968): color, 5¼ minutes

Also:

a) Footage for two films was shot but unfinished: *Zenscapes and Here and There with My Octoscope*

b) *Four American Artists* (1957, by Willard Maas and Ben Moore): b/w. [This film contains portraits of four artists, one of whom is Marie Menken, making a sand painting — RH]

Film Rental Source: Film-Makers' Cooperative, New York
Documentation: Anthology Film Archives

Sidney Peterson (1912 -)

The Potted Psalm (1946, with James Broughton): b/w, 25 minutes
The Cage (1947): b/w, 31 minutes
Horror Dream (1947): b/w, 10 minutes
Clinic of Stumble (1947): b/w, 18 minutes
Ah Nurture (1948, with Hy Hirsch): b/w, approx. 20 minutes
The Petrified Dog (1948): b/w, 19 minutes
Mr. Frenhofer and the Minotaur (1948): b/w, 21 minutes
The White Rocker (1949): b/w, approx. 20 minutes
The Lead Shoes (1949): b/w, 18 minutes
Adagio For Election Day (1949): b/w, 18 minutes
Blunden Harbor (1952): b/w, 20 minutes
Chocolate Factory (1952): b/w, 20 minutes
Doll Hospital (1952): b/w, 20 minutes
Vein Stripping (1952): b/w, 25 minutes
Architectural Millinery (1954): b/w, 7 minutes
Manhole Covers (1954): b/w, 9 minutes
Japanese House (1955): b/w, 20 minutes
Man In a Bubble (1981): b/w, 16 minutes

Also:

Scripts for 12 UPA animated films (1950s)
Fantasia II (1957-58, script, storyboard for Walt Disney): never made

Film Rentals: Film-Makers' Cooperative
Documentation: Anthology Film Archives

Index